Praise for

Garden-pe

D0174558

3|9|15

DISCARD

"*Garden-pedia* does something for me that most other books do not; it takes the intimidation out of this calming, joyous hobby as well as simplifies the language of plant science and makes us a little smarter. All books should be as useful, fun and functional. I would not be without this book."

~ **Dr. Allan M. Armitage,** Professor Emeritus of Horticulture,
University of Georgia, Athens;
author of numerous books, including *Armitage's Garden Perennials*;
co-founder, Association of Specialty Cut Flower Growers

"Gosh we like to make it complicated, using all those botanical and Latin names. Don't worry, Maria Zampini and Pam Bennett are here to save the day. With their new book, *Garden-pedia*, they have taken a sometimes confusing topic and turned it into an easy, enjoyable armchair read. These two ladies bring a wealth of down-to-earth, roll-up-your-sleeves-and-let's-get-planting experience to the table. Help is at hand."

~ **Nicholas Staddon,** Director of New Plant Introductions, Monrovia Growers

"Easy to read but hard to put down. Maria Zampini and Pam Bennett have made the science of horticulture easy to understand. For the professional horticulturalist, this book is a great reminder of the need to connect with consumers in a way that encourages them to garden. This book should be on every plant lover's required reading list."

~ **Michael V. Geary,** CAE, President & CEO, AmericanHort

"Gardening shouldn't be complicated. If you've ever felt adrift in a sea of gardening terms, this book is your lighthouse. Finally, a guide to gardening that breaks down some of the most confusing terms to 'everyday-speak'."

~ **Joe Lamp'l,** Executive Producer and Host: Growing a Greener World®, Founder and CEO: The joe gardener® Company

"Gardening is full of jargon, whether you do it professionally or pursue it as a hobby. Maria and Pam have written an enlightening and entertaining book that sifts through the words and their meanings for the benefit of gardeners everywhere."

~ **Kelly Norris,** award-winning author, Horticulture Manager, Greater Des Moines Botanical Garden

"Too many of us in the horticulture world get caught up in complex terminology when talking about plants and gardening, which may scare people off unnecessarily. This book is a great A-Z guide that makes turning your outdoor space into something beautiful less daunting. So don't be afraid to try your hand at gardening; this book breaks it down into easy-to-understand terms to make it all more understandable and approachable. Happy Gardening!"

~ **Diane Blazek,** Executive Director, All-America Selections/National Garden Bureau

"*Garden-pedia* is a handy and welcome reference book. The clear, jargon-free terms and accompanying photos and tips will boost the knowledge and confidence of all gardeners. Bennett and Zampini have done the gardening world a big favor with this practical reference."

~ **Jon Traunfeld,** Extension Specialist, University of Maryland Extension

"Leave it up to the 'Queens of Green' to bring both hobby and professional gardeners together, speaking and understanding the same gardening lingo. *Garden-pedia* is easy to read, easy to understand, and easy to use as a reference; now that's my kind of easy reading. Well done, Maria Ann and Pamela Jean! (Don't forget to add 'yardening' to *Garden-pedia II.*)"

~ **Ron Wilson,** Marketing Manager, Natorp's, radio host of "In the Garden with Ron Wilson," speaker, personal yardboy

"Remind me, where are the stolon and rhizome located?"
"Where do I find the petiole?"
"As an instructor for the Extension Master Gardener program, the hardest part of teaching is all of the garden terminology. In the past there has not been a convenient way to retrieve common-sense definitions of horticulture terms quickly and accurately. Pam and Maria have done just that with ***Garden-pedia***!

"I look forward to sharing this with all of my current Extension Master Gardeners and garden friends and incorporating it into my educational materials for future classes. Thanks to Pam and Maria, we now have a fun, convenient, and comprehensive way to learn the correct meaning of all those gardening terms we have, at times, scratched our heads and wondered, 'What does that mean?'"

~ **Terri L. James**, Extension Horticulturalist,
Nebraska Extension Master Gardener Program, University of Nebraska-Lincoln

"I have just finished a "must have" book called ***Garden-pedia***, and one that you will use as a reference book as long as you garden. Pam and Maria put it all together in a way that everyone from beginner to experienced gardener gets the information in an informative and concise way... I have been looking for a book like this for a long time!"

~ **Stephanie Cohen**, "The Perennial Diva"

"What a great resource! ***Garden-pedia*** is a fun, easy-to-read gardening book that serves as a valuable tool for all gardeners, from novice to trained professional. Maria and Pam are two of Ohio's most knowledgeable experts and sought-after speakers on gardening, so this book is sure to be a hit."

~ **Kevin Thompson**, Executive Director, Ohio Nursery & Landscape Association

"Having extensive experience in both the professional horticulture world as well as the home gardener realm, Maria Zampini and Pam Bennett join forces to serve up their collective knowledge to the rest of us. How nice that this guide gives us just what we need – an understandable and concise handbook of horticultural help."

~ **Kylee Baumle**, garden writer, blogger at Our Little Acre,
co-author of *Indoor Plant Décor: the Design Stylebook for Houseplants*

"Wow! Maria and Pam are the dynamic duo of the green industry. They have a real passion for plants and we are lucky that they are putting what they know into print. It is exciting to know we will have *Garden-pedia* as our resource, written in terms that are user-friendly for those in the green industry, those with a green thumb, and those with a new-found love of gardening. I can't wait to have a copy in my library!"

~ **Sandy Munley,** Executive Director, Ohio Landscape Association

"Maria Zampini and Pam Bennett speak just the right lingo to help new and experienced gardeners understand the language of horticulture."

~ **Jo Ellen Meyers Sharp,** author, editor, speaker, *Indianapolis Star* garden columnist; Secretary, Garden Writers Association

"*Garden-pedia* is the perfect gift for the garden enthusiast who has everything."

~ **Wes Fleming,** Managing Director, Fleming's Nurseries, Australia

"*Garden-pedia* is a breath of fresh air... a must-own manual that should be a reference guide for every single person that dabbles in the garden, to gain a broader depth and understanding of how to speak the language of gardening. Pam and Maria's unique style makes complicated topics easy to understand and use. There are way too many sources of gardening information full of garden geek language that leaves you more confused after you read it than before you started... Pam and Maria's contribution to the world of gardening is unrivaled, tireless and filled with inner passion and endless enthusiasm."

~ **Mark Webber,** host of "Garden Talk" on News95.7 WHIO, and AM 1290, Dayton, Ohio

"For the multitudes of frustrated gardeners who are befuddled by biennials, confused by cross-pollination, lost in Latin translation, mystified by micronutrients and perplexed by propagation: *Garden-pedia* will solve your problems! Authors Maria Zampini and Pam Bennett wade through the confusing jargon and present easy-to-understand terms for gardeners."

~ **Kelli Rodda,** Editor, *Nursery Management* magazine

"Maria and Pam have bridged the gap for the home gardener to help them understand what the professionals are REALLY saying. A must-have for anyone who gardens!"

~ **Denise Schreiber,** Mrs. Know It All of "The Organic Gardeners" radio show, author of *Eat Your Roses...Pansies, Lavender and 49 other Delicious Flowers*; Region 2 Director, Garden Writers Association

"This cool, user-friendly garden dictionary will quickly become your go-to guide! Bravo to veteran plantswomen Maria and Pam for writing this fun, informative, concise book."

~ **Tracy DiSabato-Aust,** garden communicator and best-selling author

"As longtime designers and horticulturalists, we have made it a priority to keep our horticultural tech-speak understandable for the everyday gardener. But a quick glance through *Garden-pedia* showed us that not only were we not up to date, but there were also some critical gaps in our knowledge! We continue to learn every year and with the great guidance of this handy book, we will be doing it in style. This is a book that will appeal to all gardeners regardless of how much dirt they have under their fingernails. Now, that makes it 'our' kind of book!"

~ **Karen Chapman** and **Christina Salwitz,** co-authors of *Fine Foliage*; Karen owns Le Jardinet garden and design company, Christina is The Personal Garden Coach

"I heartily endorse this book for new and experienced gardeners alike... The authors have created a visually appealing, clear and concise reference book. It should have a place in everyone's library who is interested in gardening. It is noteworthy that Pam Bennett has chosen to donate half of her sales proceeds to support the Ohio State Master Gardener program."

~ **Lelia Scott Kelly, Ph.D.,** Extension Professor of Horticulture, Consumer Horticulture Specialist, Mississippi State University Extension Service

"I am impressed that the authors have created such a wonderful resource for beginning gardeners, Extension Master Gardeners, and experienced horticulturists. A valuable tool."

~ **Jayla Fry,** Texas Master Gardener Coordinator, Texas A&M AgriLife Extension Service

"As an Extension professional I can see that we're currently experiencing a huge resurgence in homeowners coming back to the garden and landscape. Whether it's to grow some (or all) of their own fresh vegetables or to create a backyard habitat for that relaxing 'stay-cation,' gardeners of all skill levels have questions. I help to answer these questions on a daily basis. But like any industry, horticulture has a jargon all its own. Many gardeners I have spoken with have commented that there needs to be a garden dictionary/encyclopedia-type book available.

"*Garden-pedia* is that easy-to-read garden reference. With busy lifestyles, the home gardeners need concise, to-the-point information... I envision home gardeners considering Garden-pedia in the same light as sharing garden information with the authors over the backyard fence."

~ **Dr. Gary R. Bachman,** Associate Extension/Research Professor of Horticulture and radio and TV host of "Southern Gardening"; Coastal Research and Extension Center, Mississippi State University

"*Garden-pedia* is exactly what I have been looking for. Pam Bennett and Maria Zampini use clever illustrations and clear definitions in layman's terms that make even the most arcane horticultural jargon understandable."

~ **Lucy Bradley,** State Master Gardener Coordinator and Extension Specialist, Urban Horticulture, North Carolina State University

"At last, a book in simple terms and rich in colorful graphics that is just perfect for the new gardener or for the veteran gardener who wants a handy up-to-date reference. *Garden-pedia* authors Pam Bennett and Maria Zampini use their wealth of horticultural knowledge and experience to explain in simple language the most common garden terms and how each term is used in the garden. Concise and with beautiful illustrations, *Garden-pedia* is an easy read for the novice or experienced gardener. A must-have addition for everyone's home garden library!

"I am excited to share this book with colleagues, Master Gardeners and the gardening public in Illinois!"

~ **Monica David,** University of Illinois Extension Master Gardener Coordinator

Garden-pedia

Garden-pedia

An A-to-Z Guide to Gardening Terms

Pamela Bennett   Maria Zampini

st. lynn's
press

PITTSBURGH

CLEARVIEW
LIBRARY DISTRICT

Garden-pedia
An A-to-Z Guide to Gardening Terms

Copyright © 2015 Pamela Bennett and Maria Zampini

All rights reserved. No part of this book may be reproduced, stored, or transmitted in any form without permission in writing from the publisher, except by a reviewer who may quote brief passages for review purposes.

ISBN-13: 978-0-9892688-4-4

Library of Congress Control Number: 2014944843
CIP information available upon request

First Edition, 2015

St. Lynn's Press . POB 18680 . Pittsburgh, PA 15236
412.466.0790 . www.stlynnspress.com

Design Concept – Dawn Hummel
Layout – Holly Rosborough
Editor – Catherine Dees
Editorial intern – John Gordon

Cover photo: John Lewis, JLPN, Inc.
A complete listing of photo credits for the book can be found on page 191.

Printed in Canada
On certified FSC recycled paper using soy-based inks

This title and all of St. Lynn's Press books may be purchased for educational, business, or sales promotional use. For information please write:
Special Markets Department . St. Lynn's Press . POB 18680 . Pittsburgh, PA 15236

10 9 8 7 6 5 4 3 2 1

DEDICATIONS

❧

from Pam

First, this book is dedicated to my husband, Rick, who is my rock and biggest supporter. "Take one thing at a time" got me through some tough times! It's also dedicated to the rest of my family, friends and colleagues who always support me no matter how crazy my ideas. To the many Master Gardener Volunteers around the world – you are an amazing group of dedicated people who not only give back to your community by teaching others about gardening, but you are always so eager to learn and are always seeking additional knowledge. To my co-author Maria – thanks for inviting me to be a part of the special adventure! And finally, this book is for my dad and mom: for Dad, who has encouraged me to write a book ever since I started writing about gardening in 1992; and for Mom, for getting me my first job in horticulture that stirred my passion. Thanks for your encouragement, Mom and Dad!

DEDICATIONS

from Maria

With much love and deep gratitude to my father, Jim Zampini, who is my business partner, best friend, mentor, cheerleader and fellow hortaholic day-in and day-out – how lucky can one girl be?!; to my mother, Margaret Zampini, for her behind-the-scenes, never-ending strength and support of both me and my family; to my family and friends (and definitely my co-author Pam Bennett), for their unselfish assistance, encouragement and belief in me, especially when I had just about lost all faith in myself; and lastly, to Paul Kelly, who gently prodded me along until I finally said "yes" to writing this book and making my simple idea a reality.

TABLE of CONTENTS

INTRODUCTION
How Garden-pedia *came to be*

I [Maria] was born and raised in the world of plants, having grown up on (and eventually running) my family's 1,000-acre wholesale nursery and retail garden center businesses. During these years, whether I was working wholesale or retail, I noticed a common denominator: many of the wonderful people we hired and added to our staff had no background, let alone formal training, in the field of horticulture. There was a lot of green-industry plant jargon they had never heard before and they had to try and learn it as quickly as possible to do their job. It was always in the back of my mind to create a section in our company manual for "hort lingo," but for a variety of reasons it never became a reality. Yet my observation kept me thinking...someday.

My professional career changed course and I began to write more frequently for industry trade journals and consumer gardening magazines. As I wrote articles – in particular those directed to home gardeners – I often wondered how gardeners managed to wade through unknown terminology to understand what these new words meant. My idea of creating a book of gardening terms turned into an itch that needed scratching.

I went to my friend and colleague Pam Bennett at The Ohio State University and ran my book idea past her. She grew the idea further (bad pun intended); she thought a book of this type would also be useful for Master Gardener Volunteers, as well the younger generation who are just starting to garden. Knowing we had similar conversational writing styles, I asked her to join me on this adventure that has become *Garden-pedia*.

Getting beyond the "what" to the "why" and "how"

We had both had the same experiences when researching terms we didn't know, whether it was for a written article or to be used when teaching: the definitions we came across were dry and technical in nature. It made for painful, boring reading. Sometimes, the definition created more questions than answers; other times, the definition was just that – a definition, but it didn't include real life examples that a gardener could easily relate to. We aimed to fix that.

One of our biggest challenges was that there are so many words that we could have picked to include in this book. Horticulture and gardening covers a broad area of topics – from ornamental plants, fruits and vegetables, tropical plants, seed, sod, soil, to everything in-between. Each of these topic areas can be broken down even further. What to do? Our approach was to look at the most common terms that people ask us about in our daily travels, presentations and classes. Now, after countless back-and-forth phone calls, emails, and conversations, we think we have come up with an easy-reference definition book that clearly explains more than 300 of the most useful garden terms – chosen for the one purpose of getting you gardening with confidence.

So yes, there could be terms you feel we missed. If so, let us know! We want you to keep us on our toes. Contact us with additional words that you feel are important and we can consider adding to our next edition. Challenge us to define some of those terms that are difficult to define. Believe us, there were some gardening terms that even with all our years of practice, we struggled with putting the term on paper (see the definition for shade!).

Finally, we want you to know that the information in this book is drawn from our own combined 77 years (holy cow, maybe we should add those years again – we aren't that old) of personal experience in horticulture and our ongoing dedication and passion to helping gardeners be better informed with sound gardening information based on science.

Our wish for you

The ancient Greek playwright Aeschylus said, "From a small seed a mighty trunk may grow." Our greatest hope is that this book helps you build a strong foundation for gardening – for your own personal pleasure or as the base for some level of a career in the green industry – and inspires you to keep digging deeper to learn more.

In closing, have fun, get dirty, learn lots, live long, play in the rain; and may your garden or your gardening career prosper.

Maria and Pam

A FEW WORDS about LATIN and COMMON NAMES

Being horticulturists, we understand the value of using scientific Latin names when it comes to talking about a specific plant species. There is one scientific Latin name assigned per plant species and that one name is recognized worldwide. No room for confusion. When talking to green industry professionals, we attempt to use the Latin name as often as possible, especially when

Gailardia x grandiflora (blanketflower)

ordering plants for a job or for growing in the nursery. This ensures that both parties are referring to the same plant.

However, *Garden-pedia* is not only for people in the industry; it's for everyone, including (maybe even especially) the gardening beginner. So, how to keep it simple enough and accurate enough, and not clutter the pages with too much scientific Latin? And why not just use common names all the time? Because sometimes one plant can have many common names, depending on the region of the country or world in which it is growing. There are a good number of plants that don't even have a common name (and people make up common names as they go along, too!). Let us give you an example: Someone walks into the garden center and tells the clerk they want to purchase a red maple. Does

Acer palmatum 'Crimson Queen' (cutleaf Japanese maple)

the garden clerk sell them a red maple *(Acer rubrum)*, or a crimson king red maple *(Acer platanoides* 'Crimson King'), or even a Japanese red maple *(Acer palmatum* 'Ruby Red')? Clearly, common names don't always get you to the plant you want. In this case, a little Latin is just what you need.

As good horticulturists, we know we should use scientific Latin names for all plants throughout this book. We wrestled (not literally!) with this issue for some time and this is what we have decided. For the purposes of this book, we will use the scientific Latin name as often as possible and as necessary for clarity, accompanied by the common name – e.g., *Quercus alba* (white oak) – especially when we are talking about only one or two plants. But if we have a whole list of plants within a term definition, we will use the name most often used by gardeners. Keep in mind this might be the Latin name or the common name. Note: Scientific Latin names are always written in italics and common names in regular font.

key

When a word is shown in color and boldface (e.g., **perennial***), it will have its own listing and definition elsewhere in the book (e.g., under "*P*").*

ABIOTIC to AXIL

ABIOTIC

A non-living organism.

ACCENT/SPECIMEN

Words used to describe a plant that is bold enough to stand on its own rather than part of a mass planting.

A good way to think of accent or specimen plants is as the star – the center focus – of your garden. These are plants that are strong and interesting enough to stand alone throughout the year. They often set the theme for the rest of the garden or landscape.

For example, Japanese maples often stand alone or as the main accent plant in a garden design. We would not see a row of such trees lining a drive. On the other hand, a common perennial, albeit beautiful, like a coneflower, would not stand well alone as the main focus of a garden – they do best as part of garden design and planted in multiples.

Montgomery blue spruce

ACCLIMATION

(See: Hardening Off)

ACIDIC/ALKALINE

(See: pH)

ACID-LOVING PLANTS

Plants that grow best with a soil pH around 5.0. (See: pH)

Blueberries

AERATE

To expose to air.

This term is typically used in reference to lawns, combined with the term "core." Core aeration is recommended when soil is compact or there is a lot of thatch in the lawn. Core aeration is done with a machine (lawn aerator) that moves over the lawn and removes numerous small cores or plugs of soil. These cores of soil are left on the soil surface to break down. This practice helps to increase the amount of oxygen in the soil, which in turn increases the opportunity for healthy root growth.

AEROBIC/ANAEROBIC

Having oxygen (aerobic) or without oxygen (anaerobic).

Why is it important to know these two terms? For example, when it comes to composting, you need aerobic decomposition to occur in order for the compost process to proceed. It needs oxygen to do its work. You have an anaerobic situation with a lack of oxygen, like when the compost pile is too wet and composting shuts down and the pile begins to smell. The same when you have a bag full of wet grass clippings…well, you know the smell.

AGGREGATE

Clumps of varying sizes and shapes of primary soil particles.

The binding together of soil particles into aggregates provides soil structure. A soil with good structure is made up of aggregates of varying sizes that allow maximum space for air and water.

AGGRESSIVE

Referring to a plant's active growth behavior.

When used in horticulture terms, aggressive means that a plant is a really good grower. It's not quite invasive but it will tend to spread in the garden. When you hear this term, ask someone who has had experience with the plant in question, as this term can be very relative and dependent upon the person's perspective!

AGRICULTURE

The art and science of cultivating land for production of food and for other uses by humans.

ALKALINE

Soil with a pH of 7.1 to 14.0. (See: pH)

ALTERNATE

Generally referring to leaves that are arranged on the stem in alternating fashion. (See: Leaf Pattern)

Asimina triloba (Pawpaw)

AMEND/AMENDMENT

Anything added to your soil to improve plant growth.

In a perfect world our garden soil would be the ideal mix of sand, silt and clay, nutrients, and pH, and we would never have to amend the soil. But the reality is that more often than not, we need to help our soil by adding materials that either enhance its physical and chemical properties or provide additional nutrients. You add organic matter to the soil as an amendment in order to improve root growth and thus plant health. Amending the soil improves the structure and its ability to perform functions such as water retention, permeability, water infiltration, drainage and aeration. You can also add nutrients to amend the soil in order to improve plant growth.

Amending the soil can be accomplished through different methods. You might hear of gardeners "top dressing" their garden. This is simply adding or amending their garden with a layer, perhaps an inch or two, of organic material, such as leaf mold. Amending the soil when planting a new flowerbed, tree or shrub is also a common practice. By giving the newly installed plant an extra boost of good nutrients and rich, organic matter, the plant is more likely to take hold and thrive (not just survive) in the landscape.

Additionally, some amendments are designed to alter the pH of the soil, making it more acidic or alkaline.

ANAEROBIC

Without oxygen. (See: Aerobic/Anaerobic)

ANGIOSPERM

A flowering plant whose seeds are housed within an ovary.

Not a word you are likely to see on a plant tag or in a beginner's gardening book, huh? Angiosperms run the full gamut of garden plants, from trees and shrubs to annuals and perennials, even grasses. Gardeners do not say, "I am off to find new angiosperms for the garden!" Rather, the term is most

Asimina triloba (Pawpaw)

helpful when reading advanced garden books or keying out plants.

In contrast to angiosperm is a gymnosperm, a plant whose seeds are not protected in an ovary. Examples of gymnosperm plants include conifers such as pine, spruce, hemlock, and *Ginkgo*.

ANNUALS

Plants that complete their life cycle within one growing season.

For gardeners, mainly in northern colder winter climates, annuals are planted after spring's final frost and last until they are killed by the first frost of autumn. This is different than perennials, whose growth from the soil line above is also killed by the frost, but will re-grow from the root system the following spring.

Zinnias are one example of an annual.

ANTHER

(See: Flower)

ARBOR

A permanent garden structure, often made of wood and enhanced with lattice or other material fashioned from cut branches or strips of lumber to create an open and airy yet shady spot in the garden.

Passing under an arbor, one often feels as if they are transitioning from one area of the garden to another, from the sidewalk to the front yard or into another garden space – or, if the arbor is large enough, it can be a shady spot in the garden to sit and rest a while. As a year-round, visually interesting element in the garden, arbors are priceless. As structures on which to grow vining plants such as *Wisteria*, *Clematis* or climbing roses, arbors are a gardener's delight.

Arbors can be rustic and casual, like those in a cottage garden, or more refined and architectural in nature. They can be made of wood or even metal. More ornate arbors are often meant to stand alone without plants that may obstruct the arbor's detail work.

ARBORIST

An individual trained in the art and science of planting, caring for, and maintaining individual trees.

ARCHING

(See: Habit)

AROMATIC/FRAGRANT

Having a pleasing scent from a plant and/or its parts.

What is that wonderful scent wafting through the garden? When we think fragrance, flowers immediately come to mind. Entire gardens have been designed around fragrant plants. But not all blooms have a lovely scent to them. In fact, some flowers have a terrible smell; skunk cabbage for instance, smells like rotted meat in order to attract pollinators such as flies.

Additionally, other plants and/or certain plant parts can have a unique smell. For instance, just think of bayberry candles during the holidays. This aromatic scent is derived from the berries found on *Myrica pensylvanica*. In fact, if you employ scratch and sniff horticulture, you discover that the stem of this plant is also very fragrant. *Lindera benzoin*, commonly known as spicebush, has wood which is exactly that: spice scented. Crush *Viburnum setigerum* leaves and you'll be reminded of green peppers.

ASCENDING

Another term to describe the upright growth habit of a plant.

Calamagrostis 'Karl Foerster'

ASEXUAL

Propagation without pollination, maintaining the identity of the parent plant. (See: Clone)

AXIL

The upper angle between the leaf and stem.

BACTERIA to BUSH

BACTERIA

Single-celled organisms that cannot be seen with the unaided eye. Bacteria can be both beneficial and detrimental to plants.

BALLED & BURLAPPED

Sometimes called B&B for short – a method used for harvesting large, mature trees and shrubs where a round root ball is dug out and held intact by a large piece of burlap, which is held in place by wire, twine and/or pins, allowing the plant to safely be dug, transported and replanted in another location.

Unlike widgets, plants can't simply be pulled down off a shelf anytime you want. When it comes to digging and moving in-ground plant material from one location to another, one of the most important things you need to know is there's a small window of opportunity to accomplish this task with the highest degree of success. Most commonly, wholesale nurseries harvest plant material dug from the field in the spring and fall; in the spring before deciduous plants break bud and in the fall after a killing frost as the plants become dormant. Evergreens and conifers are harvested before they push new growth in the spring.

Yes, you can dig plants during the growing season but it requires planning and a multitude of precautions both before digging, after harvest and again after transplanting. The probability of plant loss is increased when not done in the spring or fall – even for professional growers, let alone homeowners. You can have success with summer digging and transplanting of field dug plant material; just know it is a precise process and you'll need to provide extra planning, time, and a little extra TLC.

BARE ROOT

Plants sold without soil around their roots.

These are most often dormant plants that have either been dug out of the ground or removed from a container growing pot and had the soil removed from around the roots prior to shipping to wholesale or retail customers.

Be sure to read the instructions on your bare root plant prior to planting. It's recommended that you soak the roots in water for a few hours in order to re-hydrate the root hairs so that they can begin to absorb water and nutrients quickly.

BARK

The external covering of the stems, branches and roots of woody plants – distinct from the wood itself.

Betula nigra (river birch)

BEDDING PLANTS

Usually referring to any plant that is produced and sold for planting in the landscape in a flowerbed or mass planting.

Historically, bedding plants were herbaceous plants (primarily annuals) that were grown to be used outdoors in flowerbeds for color. But today, the definition is broader and includes flowers, vegetables, biennials, herbs, ground covers and more.

BENEFICIALS

Insects that are desirable to have in the garden and landscape.

Wait! Don't kill that insect! Certain insects are highly desirable in the garden and landscape as they feed on pests that can do harm to crops and garden plants. Some insects, such as bees, are necessary for pollinating plants and are an essential component of the cycle of life.

Understanding which insects contribute to the overall health of your plants is critical to knowing which bugs need to be eradicated

Ambush bug

and which should be encouraged to stay. Monitor your garden to see if there are adequate beneficials; if so, let them do the work instead of using pesticides.

BIENNIAL

Plants that take two growing seasons to complete their lifecycle.

In the first growing season, the biennial plant will set roots and grow leaves. Typically, the plant will grow in a rosette form (a circular arrangement of leaves that are usually near the soil), remaining short and having smaller leaves than those that will appear in the second season. The plant will go through a dormant period triggered by colder temperatures (not necessarily a defined length of time), and then, in the second year, or warm season, will send up stems and leaves, flower, become pollinated, go to seed and then die. Examples of biennials are parsley, foxglove, hollyhock, and sweet William.

BIODEGRADABLE

An object that is capable of being naturally broken down or deteriorated over time by living organisms.

Biodegradable items are often made from organic substances, such as plant or animal material, or other matter similar enough in composition to be broken down naturally. An example would be a plantable pot, a type that is made of biodegradable material and can be planted (with its plant) directly into the ground – as opposed to a plastic pot, which will not biodegrade. The breaking down process can happen with or without oxygen. Oftentimes, the term "compostable" is used interchangeably with biodegradable; this is close, but not 100-percent accurate. If something is meant to be composted, it means it goes into a compost pile to be broken down into smaller pieces. Biodegradable material does not have to go into a compost pile to break down.

BIOLOGICAL CONTROL

One component of an integrated pest management strategy (see page 76) in the garden and landscape, where a gardener focuses on reducing pest populations by using natural enemies.

Natural enemies or "beneficial" insects include predators, parasites, and parasitoids. Biological control may include surveying and scouting for beneficial insects, introducing them to the landscape, or providing shelter and food for them to thrive.

BIOTIC

A living organism.

BLOOM

The opening up of a flower bud. (Also, an increase of algae in water.)

There are good blooms and not-so-good blooms. The good blooms are those that come to mind right away: the beautiful flowers in your garden in their open and peak stage (before they start to wilt and wither away). It is the bloom of a flower that breeders strive to enhance – a larger bloom, brighter bloom or a longer lasting bloom. Don't forget that the blooms are also one of the ways that a plant attracts pollinators in order to ensure longevity of the species.

Now, should you hear a gardener say in a distraught manner that they have "bloom in their pond," that is not a good thing. Oftentimes, bloom is used as shorthand for algae bloom. This is a condition in a body of water when the population density of algae increases, discoloring the water and making the once-clear garden pond not so attractive. Some blooms can change the color of the water to yellow-brown or red and may be hazardous to humans.

BOLT/BOLTING

When a plant goes to seed prematurely.

This does not mean that plants are going to pick up and run, as one new gardener thought! Warm weather sends some plants into the reproductive stage and seeds are produced. Bolting is common with garden crops that prefer cooler weather for optimal growth. Lettuce, spinach, beets, carrots, rhubarb, cabbage and others will produce flowers and seeds prematurely (before you have a chance to enjoy them). Other reasons that plants bolt include changes in day length and stresses such as lack of water or nutrients.

BONSAI

A Japanese art form that uses miniature trees growing in containers and combines art and horticulture.

The "art" is trying to take a large specimen tree and making it appear as a miniature living in a small container. The science is the right environment and growing needs to keep the plant alive. Bonsai is usually considered a hobby and can be very time-consuming but the results are museum-quality plants.

BORDER/BORDER PLANT

A plant that is used to define or divide the space between the garden and the lawn, walk, drive or another non-garden area.

This definition refers primarily to the herbaceous perennial border, which had its origins in England in the late 1800's.

At that time, borders were perennial gardens that were growing in front of a hedge that was used for the backdrop. Many plants can be border plants, so you will not see a "border plant" section in your local garden center or nursery. These plants are usually shorter plants and placed in the front of the garden area, followed by medium-height and then tall plants in the back, using the hedge for a backdrop or background. You'll find all types of plants in a border, including specimen trees or shrubs, as well as annuals, perennials, bulbs and grasses. Garden art is sometimes placed strategically throughout the planting.

BOTANY

The scientific study of plants (a botanist is a person who specializes in this field).

BRAMBLE

A shrub with thorns that is in the rose family.

Blackberries and raspberries are considered brambles.

BRANCH COLLAR

The area where the branch attaches to the trunk of a tree, sometimes visible with a little ring around the branch.

BROADCAST

To spread fertilizer over the growing area.

BROAD SPECTRUM

Pesticides that affect a wide variety of pests.

BROADLEAVED EVERGREENS

A plant with leaves year-round.

In general, broadleaved evergreens have one central vein and the leaves are often flat, broad or wide. To further clarify, broadleaved evergreens do not keep their leaves forever, as they do drop their leaves eventually, but just certain leaves. Unlike deciduous trees and plants that drop all their leaves at the end of the growing season, broadleaved evergreen plants will drop leaves at some time during the growing season, depending upon the species. They generally drop their older leaves with new leaves developing during the next growing season, ensuring that the plant is always evergreen. Examples include *Rhododendron*, azaleas, mountain laurel and *Pieris*.

Rhododendron

Mountain laurel – an example of broadleaved evergreens

BUD

An undeveloped or embryonic shoot that normally occurs in the axil (page 8) of a leaf or at the tip of a stem.

A bud may develop into a flower, leaf or branch depending on the type of bud.

BUD BREAK

(See: Leaf out)

BUDDING

A term with two definitions: one for propagation and the other for what a plant naturally does as it emerges from the cold of winter.

Technically speaking, budding is a form of propagation (specifically asexual plant reproduction) in which new plant material forms from buds from a parent plant. One would use budding versus other means of propagation when, for instance, you have a tree which does not naturally produce a good root system. You start with a liner or "baby" plant of a compatible tree (which produces a good root system) and slice a "T" into its bark. This type of liner is known as an understock. You then cut out a bud from the desired tree (with the weak root system) and insert it into the "T." That bud will mesh and bond with the liner and the new tree will grow from the bud, having a good root system supplied by the understock, with the trunk upward being the tree with other desirable characteristics intact. You are basically making one tree out of two!

As a common term in the garden, budding can be the first sign of spring as leaves, flowers and branches surrounded by bud scales (protective covering) begin to plump as the weather warms. When the plant breaks dormancy, the buds scales (or shells) fall off, allowing the flowers, leaves or stems to emerge. You will also hear the term "bud break" used when plants start to grow in the new season.

Ohio buckeye at bud break

BULB

An underground storage organ of a plant consisting of a modified underground stem and modified leaves that contain stored food for the plant.

Bulbs store food or reserves for the plant that will emerge from its center following a dormancy period. The leaves of the plant that grow from the center of the underground organ replenish the energy reserves of the plant, allowing it to go dormant and re-emerge the following season. True bulbs are tulips, daffodils, and lilies. Corms, tubers and rhizomes are also grouped under bulb-like plants.

A common desire for gardeners is to cut back the leaves once the bulb's flower has faded. When the leaves fade, they tend to look a little straggly. The best thing to do is to let these leaves grow as long as possible in order to replenish reserves for the following season. This allows good bulb growth and bloom for the next season. There is always a lot of conversation regarding the habit of "braiding" or "folding-over" the foliage in order to tidy up the garden during the period of time right after bloom. This is usually a practice done on daffodils. The surface area of the foliage is needed for photosynthesis, which produces the sugars needed for storage in the bulb for the next season's growth. When you braid or fold-over the foliage, you decrease the surface area of the foliage, thereby decreasing the surface area for photosynthesis. However, we both know of people who do this regularly and it doesn't seem to really hurt the quality of blooms. Our philosophy is to go as long as you can possibly stand the untidy look and then just when you can't take it any longer, go one more week!

Bulbs can also be forced to bloom indoors during the winter season, following an artificial and often shortened dormancy period. We enjoy beauty from such bulbs as *Amaryllis* and *Narcissus*.

BUSH

A slang term for shrub.

Forsythia

Sarraceniaceae
Sarracenia
'udith Hindle'
pitcher plant

Sarraceniaceae
Sarracenia psittacina
parrot pitcher plant, lobster-pot pitcher plant
coastal, GA & FL to MS

CAMBIUM to
CUTTING GARDEN

CAMBIUM

The tissue in the plant that produces new cells.

The cambium is found in two places in a stem; in the bud where it produces tissue that increases the length of the stem and circling the stem where it develops and increases the diameter or girth of the tree.

CANE

A hollow or pithy jointed, woody stem.

Plants that have stems that have hollow or pithy jointed woody stems are considered cane plants. The stems are called

canes. Examples of plants with canes include *Dieffenbachia* and corn plant, roses (photo bottom left), bamboo, sugar cane, brambles (blackberries, raspberries, black raspberries), among others.

CARNIVOROUS PLANT

A plant that attracts and consumes insects.

In the plant world, carnivorous plants are those that have specialized leaves or leaf parts that trap and digest insects. Common

Venus flytrap

carnivorous plants include Venus flytrap, sundews, and pitcher plants.

CHIPPING

Can refer to breaking branches or wood up into smaller pieces by a wood chipping machine.

Also – a form of propagating bulbs. (We do love our gardening vocabulary to have double meanings!)

Chipper-shredders are machines that are very useful to use if your garden and landscape produces a lot of woody plant debris (after pruning, for instance). These machines chip the wood into smaller pieces for faster breakdown during the compost process.

Chipping as a form of propagation: Some bulbs are not easy to divide to create new plants. Chipping is one way to create new bulbs and thus new plants. Have you ever dug up an older bulb and noticed that there are many new, baby bulbs forming? Those new, baby bulbs can be separated from the parent bulb and planted to start a new stand of plants identical to the parent bulb plant.

When the bulb is dormant, cut off the tip of the bulb (the area where new leaves emerge) and remove any roots without cutting the base or basal plate of the bulb. With a clean knife, cut down through the basal plate of the bulb to make 6–14 equal pieces or "chips." Apply fungicide to the chips and then dry the chips before placing them in a clean, plastic bag with a moist mixture of 50 percent perlite and 50 percent peat or vermiculite. Do not squeeze the air out of the bag before sealing. Place the bag in a dark, cold space (about 20 degrees Farenheit). In 12 weeks, you should see roots emerging from your chips. The chips are now ready for planting in a temporary growing medium of potting compost and grit (tiny gravel) in a 50/50 mix. Grow the bulbs in a cool, shady spot for the summer and then a cold frame for the winter. Repeat this process until the bulbs have reached mature planting size and are ready for garden installation. Daffodils are an example of a bulb propagated by chipping.

CHLOROPHYLL

The pigment in plants that give leaves, fruits and sometimes flowers their green color.

CHLOROSIS

A yellowing of a plant or plant foliage due to insufficient production of chlorophyll.

Chlorophyll gives leaves their green color; chlorotic leaves may appear yellow or pale yellow, oftentimes with dark green veins remaining. Many factors may cause the condition, so it is imperative to determine the cause before a proper treatment plan can be put in place.

Plants that are subjected to compacted, waterlogged or extremely dry soil may show signs of chlorosis. Plants that have damaged roots or have been treated with pesticides may also become chlorotic. The pH level of soil may also contribute to the condition, particularly for plants that don't grow well in soils with a high pH. *Quercus palustris* (pin oak), for instance, will have iron chlorosis if planted in akaline soils. The iron may be plentiful in the soil but unavailable for plant uptake due to soil pH. The best way to prevent iron chlorosis is to select the right plant for the location.

CLAY

One of the three mineral ingredients of ideal soil that gardeners strive to have in somewhat equal parts – the other two minerals being silt and sand. (See: Soil)

Technically speaking, clay soil differs from other fine-grained soils by particle size and mineralogy. Silt, a fine-grained material, tends to have larger particle sizes than clay, but smaller than sand. To put this in perspective, sand is about the size of a softball, silt is about the size of a baseball, and clay is the size of a golf ball.

To gardeners, clay is a substance that bonds well to itself, holds water, does not allow for adequate air and water movement, but is rich in nutrients. When gardeners say they have clay soil, they do not mean their soil is all clay, but that it is rich in clay and rather tricky to work and dig.

Chlorophyll gives these basil leaves their green color

CLIMBING

Plants that require a structure to support their growth habit.

Climbing plants rely on rocks, walls, arbors, and other plants to support themselves; otherwise, the plant is not able to hold itself up and will collapse and become trailing. Climbing plants use sucker-like roots and/or tendrils (think

fingers) to attach themselves and wrap around a branch, twig or other element for support. Some "climbers" can be extremely woody and heavy, so be sure to know the mature

habit of the plant that you are thinking about purchasing for an arbor or other structure. Examples include grapevines, *Clematis* and ivy.

CLOCHE

A bell-shaped glass cover that is placed over a seedling in the early season to protect it from cold temperatures and to encourage growth.

Cloche is French for "bell," as in a bell jar or dish cover. In the garden, think of it as a mini-glass greenhouse over a tender plant.

CLONE

An identical reproduction of the parent plant.

A clone is the result of asexual reproduction in which a new plant is produced without the use of seeds or spores and can be achieved any number of ways, either naturally or by gardeners. For example, strawberry plants send out runners, which take root and produce new strawberry plants identical to the parent plant. Gardeners take cuttings or leaves (such as from succulents), treat them with hormones and grow a new plant identical to the plant from which the cutting originated.

COIR

A fiber that is extracted from the husk of coconuts.

Coir has a number of uses in gardening, one being a soil amendment alternative for peat moss. Coir can be used in the garden or in container and hanging basket soilless mixes.

Long coir fibers are woven into mats or liners and then used to line wire hanging baskets.

COLD FRAME

A structure, usually covered with glass or plastic, that provides a favorable environment for growing cool-weather crops, protecting them from freezing temperatures; also used to harden-off seedlings that are started indoors.

COLD HARDY

(See: Hardiness/Hardy)

COLD SNAP

An extreme change in weather in which the temperature drops and the air becomes quite dry.

A cold snap is a weather event that strikes fear in the hearts of gardeners everywhere, especially when it occurs in early spring after a warm period that causes plants to start to grow. It provides less than ideal condition for plants and can result in cold damage to the tender new growth of plants or even death.

COMMUNITY GARDEN

A piece of land, usually in an urban setting, that is planted and tended by a group of people either collectively or in individual plots.

Community gardens can be on public or private land. There is a great deal of interest in these neighborhood gardens, especially in urban environments – as a source of food security, for greening and revitalizing neglected city spaces, and for building a sense of community. For more information, visit https://communitygarden.org/. A similar term is *urban agriculture*, or the cultivation of food in an urban area.

COMPACT

(See: Habit)

COMPANION PLANTS

Plants that grow well together and even enhance each other's ability to thrive.

In edible gardening (growing plants for harvest), companion plantings have been used for centuries. Legumes, such as beans, capture nitrogen and enhance the soil, which benefits plants such as corn. The beans do not compete with corn for nutrients and the corn provides a vertical surface on which the beans can grow. Add a cover crop like squash, which shades the soil, keeping it moist as well as blocking out weeds and you have a companion garden.

Additionally, some companion plants are used to attract pollinators to increase crop yield or to attract beneficial insects, which prey on insects that are harmful to the crops. Another example is taller plants, which will provide needed shade for shorter plants, and grasses planted in fruit tree groves to keep the soil cool and conserve water.

In regard to companion plants in ornamental gardening, it is not uncommon to see suggestions of companion plants for a particular plant written on plant tags or in popular gardening magazines. If you are shopping online, a nursery may recommend companion plants for the *Hosta* you just added to your shopping cart. Savvy nurseries create vignettes of plants that work well together in the garden. In ornamental gardening, companion plants are selected for aesthetic purposes. The foliage of one plant may highlight and contrast well with another plant such as the white variegation of a *Hosta* that adds brightness and a bit of softness next to the rougher textured and darker color of *Rodgersia*. Companion plants extend

the bloom and visual interest of a garden. Plants are selected that bloom at different times or bring interesting colors of foliage, bark or texture to the garden. For example, a tall stand of the ornamental grass *Calamagrostis* 'Karl Foerster' is striking behind a swath of purple coneflowers in bloom; and once the blooms are spent, the unique architecture and the intense red seeds and orange leaves of the sumac keeps the drama of the garden extended well into fall. Companion planting with ornamentals is all about highlighting the best qualities of the plants within a design.

COMPOST/COMPOSTING

Decomposed organic matter that is incorporated back into the garden and landscape in order to improve soils.

Compost is oftentimes referred to as "black gold" by gardeners and is a rich organic matter that can be used to improve garden soil. The composting process is both an art and a science, with the art relying on the combination of materials that will lead to quicker breakdown (the science).

COMPOST TEA

A low-nutrient liquid extract that results from placing finished compost in water and extracting the beneficial organisms and compounds. (See: Compost)

CONE

Botanically speaking, the conical (more or less) multiple fruit of pines, firs, cedars and others.

Some plants that are considered conifers produce fruits that are referred to as cones. Since these are the fruits of these plants, they are also the reproductive organs of the plant.

CONICAL

A cone-like plant shape where the base is the widest point of the plant and it becomes narrower or more slender towards the top.

Certain plants grow naturally in the form of a cone shape, such as many hemlocks, pines or spruces. The shape can be refined with select pruning. In other cases, as with some trees, they are trimmed to assume a conical outline.

CONIFER

A group of plants, usually though not always an evergreen, that is cone-bearing.

All conifers are woody plants, but some are considered trees while others are shrubs. Pine, spruce, larch and weeping cedar can all be considered "trees." Shrubs would include bird's nest spruce, *Taxus*

and mugho pine. The deciduous tree *Ginkgo* is also a conifer. Many people lump all of the cones produced by conifers into the pine cone category, however, they aren't all considered pine cones. You can really impress people with your plant geekiness if you call them correctly – spruce cones, cedar cones, etc.

CONTAINER

Any vessel or object used to hold soil and grow plants.

In terms of producing plants, black or nursery-branded pots or hanging baskets are examples of containers used by wholesale growers to grow larger or

"finished" plants. Smaller, baby plants, referred to as "liners," can be grown in flats which contain small "cells" of soil.

In landscaping terms, garden containers are used to grow plants for many reasons. They are primarily used to add to the landscape in areas where a garden in the ground might not be possible.

Containers have evolved well beyond traditional, nondescript clay pots. Anything that can hold soil is fair game with today's gardeners. Old buckets, coffee cans, apothecary jars, shoes, even wooden pallets lined with fabric, are used to contain soil and grow plants. Keep in mind that containers may need additional watering because they are above-ground and exposed to a harsher environment than a flowerbed. If you use a growing medium or soilless mix, you must also fertilize on a regular basis to keep plants looking their best *(See: Fertilizer).*

COOL SEASON CROPS

Plants that not only prefer, but thrive during cooler temperature growing conditions.

Cool season crops do best when grown in temperatures that are about 15 degrees less than plants requiring warmer growing conditions. Many vegetables fall into the "cool season crop" category, meaning they have edible leaves or roots, which, if grown during warmer months, may become less desirable in texture and take on a bitter taste. Cabbage, broccoli, lettuce and spinach are examples of cool season edibles. In addition, cool

season vegetables bolt when temperatures rise.

Certain annuals may also be referred to as "cool season plants." Examples include *Violas* or  pansies (photo), which thrive in early spring and fall but cannot tolerate the hot, dry summer months.

COOPERATIVE EXTENSION SERVICE

A nationwide network of educational and research outreach services – a valuable resource for research-based, unbiased information.

The Smith-Lever Act of 1914 established a system that has federal and local governments and land grant universities in the U.S. cooperating to provide research-based education to the citizens of the state. It is the outreach arm of the land grant university and takes the research from the university to the people in order to improve the quality of life. The beginning of the Extension system saw on-farm research and training, home economics educational programs for the farm wives and 4-H programs for youth. Today, the outreach continues in the U.S., offering a wide variety of programs and services – related to agriculture, youth development, and family and consumer sciences.

CORM

A compressed stem that contains stored food with a bud on the top. Crocus and gladiolus are examples of corms.

COTTAGE GARDEN

A style of garden that is simplistic and free-flowing, with jumbles and mixes of plants, leading to a lot of color in the garden.

These gardens aren't necessarily designed, so to speak, but rather are mixes of favorite plants.

The plants are tightly packed together with as many as possible in a small space; "charming  disarray" is a good term to describe the cottage garden. Many of the plants are grown from seed and easily reseed each season. Cottage gardens came to the U.S. from England.

COVER CROP

A crop that is planted by gardeners with the intention of improving soil health – often referred to as green manure.
(See: Green Manure)

In farming, cover crops are used to prevent erosion and loss of soil. Cover crops are typically planted in late summer and then tilled into the soil in the spring right before planting the garden. Typical plants for a garden cover crop include annual ryegrass, winter rye, winter wheat, oats, white clover, sweet clover, buckwheat, and hairy vetch.

CREEPING

A type of growth habit where the plant spreads out and away from its center, often along the ground or on landscape structures such as a stone wall.

Oftentimes, creeping plants form a dense cover; as such, they make an excellent groundcover that will conserve water by shading the soil and minimizing germination of weed seed.

CROP ROTATION

The practice of growing a succession of different crops on the same land in a particular sequence, in order to deter weeds, pests and diseases, and to preserve or increase the health of the soil.

CROWN

The top of the head of a tree.
Or, the part of the plant where the stem meets the roots.

We can easily identify the top of a tree, but what about the other "crown," the one at the base of a plant? It is the place where the above-ground portion of the plant (stems, leaves, branches) meets the below-surface parts (the roots). If the crown of a plant is placed

below soil grade, the plant may struggle or even die.

CULTIVAR

A plant that is bred so that it has a desired characteristic or trait that can be duplicated and maintained through propagation (i.e., a cultivated variety). The cultivar is non-italicized and in single quotations, after the Latin name. For instance this photo shows Heuchera 'Fireworks'.

CULTURE/ CULTURAL PRACTICES

The basic needs and conditions that a plant requires in order to thrive.

Gardeners need to learn the cultural requirements of a plant in order to know if a plant will thrive in a specific location in the garden. For instance, the cultural requirements of a rose includes placing them in full sun, providing water, fertilizer, and good air circulation, as well as pruning them back in the spring season.

CURB APPEAL

The outside appearance of a property – especially important when discussing selling and marketing a home in order to draw in prospective buyers and make them want to take a closer look. The contents of your landscape can play a part in this.

Curb appeal can come from new shutters, a freshly painted door, front porch with comfy chairs, flowering planters, a nicely edged front lawn and a front garden that is well tended, blooming and looks easy to care for. It can also be as simple as a fresh coat of mulch around the house and flowerbeds. As gardeners, we often forget that not everyone is as enamored with gardening as we are. Where we see a

fabulously rich, generously-sized garden, others may see tedious hours spent doing yard work. If you are planning gardens based on curb appeal, be certain to keep in mind how the not-so-experienced gardener will view them. When it comes to curb appeal and gardens, bigger isn't always better!

If you're a novice gardener looking to sell your house, consider evaluating your home's curb appeal before posting that for-sale sign. A "curb appeal clean-up" has been proven to increase how fast your home sells and can positively affect the amount it sells for, too!

CUTTING

A piece of plant that is cut from the main plant in order to develop or propagate a new plant.

A cutting is referred to the small portion of a plant that is removed from the stock plant in order to propagate the stock (mother) plant. The cutting is usually taken from the growing tip of the stock plant. The cutting is then stuck in a growing medium that is specific for root development. The cuttings need to be babied and coddled until the new roots form. Spraying a mist of water helps to keep the cuttings moist until the roots develop and take in water.

CUTTING GARDEN

A type of garden planting in which the majority of the plants are cut and used in arrangements.

If you want a cutting garden in your landscape, select those plants that are recommended to be used as cut flowers in a vase or dried and used in flower arrangements. The best flowers for cutting gardens are those that have blooms that will last for a few days in a vase or will dry nicely, to be used in a longer lasting arrangement.

DAYS TO MATURITY to DWARF

DAYS TO MATURITY/HARVEST

The length of time from when the seed germinates to the harvesting of the fruit.

If you are a gardener who likes to start plants from seeds, whether it's indoors or outside in the garden, you start by purchasing a seed packet. The packet will have listed on it the days to maturity for that plant.

DBH

(See: Girth)

DEADHEADING

Removing the dead blooms from a plant.

Once a bloom dies, it should be removed from the plant. When you deadhead

annual plants, it helps to keep them blooming throughout the growing season. Deadheading in the perennial garden is necessary to keep the garden looking its best and deadheading roses will encourage another flush of blooms as well as make the plant look better. However, deadheading trees or shrubs is not usually necessary, as the new growth the next season covers the dead blooms. Go ahead and deadhead trees and shrubs if the dead blooms are unsightly for a long period of time - but know this, it's a lot of work!

DEADLEAFING

*The act of removing dead leaves
from a plant.*

Deadleafing is similar to deadheading except in this case, you are removing dead or dying leaves. This keeps the plant looking its best and may help to prevent disease from spreading.

DEAD SPOT

*An area of your lawn or on a plant
that is, yes, dead.*

A rather self-explanatory phrase, dead spot is actually most often used when referring to a brown or dead area in the turf or lawn. A dead spot can be the result of many culprits, including: critters (moles or voles), insects or disease, damage from pesticides/fungicides, fertilizer burn in the lawn (such as dropping or spilling a pile of fertilizer on the grass or an improperly calibrated fertilizer spreader), spilled gasoline, thin soil that dries out too quickly – or any other of a host of culprits.

As with other unfortunate situations in gardening, it is not always clear how to rectify the problem. You may want to do a bit of exploratory digging; check if there is patch of old cement from the home's construction, building debris or perhaps an old tree stump. Take a look at the leaf blades of the plants near the dead spot to see if there are any signs of insect or disease problems. Low or high spots in the lawn can cause wet or dry spots, as can improperly installed irrigation systems. Look at the area where the dead spot is located; does it have something to do with the heat from the sidewalk drying the soil? The plus side of gardening is that it is an art *and* a science, which means with enough investigation there is always a solution! You can contact your local Extension office or garden experts to help you identify the cause of the problem as well as how to fill in with new seed.

DECIMUOUS

Referring to trees and shrubs that drop all of their leaves at the end of a growing season.

Thanks to deciduous trees and shrubs, we enjoy all those spectacular fall foliage colors.

Oh yeah, and raking up all those leaves once they fall off the tree, which believe it or not, we love to do! If you don't have massive amounts of leaves, run the lawn mower over them in the fall and allow them to break down into your lawn. Look at the positive side to raking leaves and use broken-down leaves as leaf mold!

DECIDUOUS CONIFERS

Conifers that have needles that drop the end of the growing season.

Don't be fooled! Some gardeners may mistakenly believe deciduous conifers have died when they see all of the needles drop from the tree in the fall. In fact, the tree is simply going dormant. Examples of such plants are larch, dawn redwood and baldcypress. We have heard horror stories (to us tree-huggers) of people cutting these trees down because they thought they were dead! Identify the species first before taking action.

DEEP WATERING

Adding water to the garden soil so that it is saturated well below the top layer (typically 8 inches or more).

Deep watering is a better alternative to frequent, shallow watering. With deep watering, enough water is applied to the specific plant or area so as to saturate well below the garden surface. Plant roots grow in the top 12-15 inches of soil, depending on the plant. Shallow watering leads to shallow roots, where plants' roots are only in the upper surfaces of the soil, making them susceptible to drying out between watering. Keep in mind that shallow watering doesn't result in the plant roots growing up to the surface and seeking the water. Plant roots don't seek water; if there isn't any water deep in the soil, they will not survive.

To deep water, set a sprinkler or soaker hose on an area

for an extended period of time, longer for clay soil, less for sandy soil. To check how much water was delivered, take a trowel and gently dig down into the soil area to determine the actual depth of the water.

DEER RESISTANT

A plant that deer don't usually eat.

Gardeners in areas that have high populations of deer worry about these critters eating their valued landscape plants. There are some plants that the deer absolutely love (we call these "deer candy!") and there are those that they don't like or don't tend to bother. The latter are considered deer resistant plants.

Many online sites list plants that are considered to be deer resistant. However, keep in mind that if deer are really hungry and food isn't easily available, they may eat a plant that is considered deer resistant. Think about a deer resistant plant list as suggested plants that deer don't like, rather than plants they absolutely won't eat.

DESICCATION

The decrease or complete loss of moisture by plants.

Plants may wilt, droop, or die as their water content becomes too low. Drought conditions, hot, dry winds and/or constant full sun can cause this to occur. Plant dessication occurs in winter months on evergreens when the soil is frozen and plants can't take in moisture to replace what's lost to wind. On some occasions, forgetful plant owners who fail to water plants, especially potted plants, will lead the plants to drop their leaves. Don't be ashamed to admit it; we've all toasted a plant or two (or more) in our lives!

DETERMINATE

Referring to tomatoes where growth of the plant is limited.

If veggie gardening is what gets you out to the garden, the term determinate is valuable to know, especially when discussing tomatoes. Determinate tomatoes are those that grow to a certain height. Often called bush tomatoes, they are, as a result of this growth habit, shorter, do not require staking, and ripen all of their fruit at one time. Helpful hint: determinate tomatoes should not be pruned!

On the flip side, we have indeterminate or climbing or vining tomatoes. These plants continue to grow and set new fruit until frost, disease, or other circumstances causes the plant to die. As a result, these tomato plants do require caging, staking, or pruning, and will continue to produce fresh fruit and flowers throughout the growing season.

DIBBLER

A simple tool used by gardeners to poke a hole in the ground.

It's usually about 6 inches long and about ½-inch in width, with a pointed end to poke in the ground. It is frequently used in transplanting seedlings from the seedbed to a larger container.

DIOECIOUS

Plants that have only male or only female flowers on a single plant.

There are many ways in which plants reproduce and when it comes to pollination, male and female parts in a flower are necessary. In some plants, the male and female parts actually occur on two different plants of the same species.

If you are purchasing a plant specifically for its fruit, for instance, you need to know this factor so you can purchase one of each sex. Hollies are a great

'Red Sprite' winterberry

example, because you need a male and a female in order to get the holly berries that we love to use for decorating during the holidays. *Ilex meserveae* 'Blue Boy' and 'Blue Girl' is a case in point. Luckily, only one male plant is needed to fertilize multiple female plants, so just one 'Blue Boy' will do the job for many 'Blue Girls'!

In addition, when designing public spaces or even in your own backyard, knowing if a plant is male or female is most helpful when the fruit of the female plant is less than desirable. A notorious example is the female *Ginkgo* tree, which produces fruit with an offensive odor (smells like dog poop to us!). In this case, a nice stand of male trees is preferable.

DIRECT SOW

Planting seeds directly into the ground, as opposed to starting them indoors under artificial light and in a growing medium.

DISEASE

Any abnormal condition in a plant that interferes with its growing processes.

Diseases in plants can be caused by pathogens, parasite, and unfavorable environmental, genetic, or nutritional factors. Types of diseases include blight, powdery mildew, leaf spot, stem and fruit rot, and many more.

DISEASE RESISTANT/ DISEASE TOLERANT

(See: Resistant/Tolerant)

DISEASE TRIANGLE

The three factors needed for plant disease to occur: a susceptible host plant, a plant pathogen, and the right environmental conditions.

Understanding and managing plant diseases requires an awareness of the three components of the disease triangle:

- A susceptible host plant
- A plant pathogen (a disease-causing organism)
- The right environmental conditions

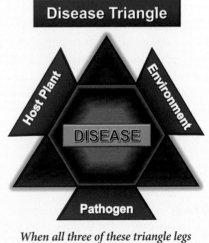

When all three of these triangle legs occur at the same time, the opportunity exists for a disease to develop.

To understand the components of the triangle, let's take a look at black spot on roses. Black spot is a common rose disease and occurs when there is a rose plant (susceptible host), the fungus *Diplocarpon rosae* (pathogen), and daily moisture on the leaf surface for around 7 hours with temperatures around 65°F (environment). When all three conditions are present in the garden, the disease occurs. Manipulating one of the three components can sometimes help in managing a disease. For instance, keeping moisture off the leaf surface when watering; planting roses in full sun so that overnight dews dry off quickly in the morning; and providing good air circulation around the plants with proper pruning and spacing – all help regulate the environment and stave off possible disease.

DORMANT/DORMANCY

A plant in an inactive growth state.

A dormant plant is one that is not growing and any of its potential areas of growth, such as branches or flowers, are protected by buds or scales. Plants become dormant during the colder, winter months and in some regions, during the drier seasons. When the seasons change, becoming warmer or wetter, a plant's dormancy is broken and is sometimes called "breaking dormancy," i.e., when the buds burst forth with flowers or leaves.

DOUBLE DIGGING

*A method used to prepare
the garden bed for planting.
(See: Hardpan)*

We bow down to anyone who has prepared a garden bed by double digging!
Anyone who has done this knows what we
mean because it's no easy task. It's an old
English method of preparing a bed where
you dig a trench about two feet deep and
put the soil into a wheelbarrow for later.
Next to this trench, you take out the top
one foot of soil (about a foot wide) and
place it in the bottom of the first trench,
then take the next one foot of soil from the
bottom and put it on top of the bottom soil
in the first trench. Keep doing this until
you are either dead tired or the garden bed
is ready to go! *Hint:* you will be dead tired
anyway, but hats off to you!

DRAINAGE

*Referring to how well the soil allows
water to drain through it.*

Good drainage is absolutely a must for
plants. Why is that? Plant roots require
oxygen in order to thrive, but if the soil
environment is saturated with water, there
is no pore space for oxygen – and roots
die. Poorly drained soils remain wet for
much of the year.

A quick and dirty check to see if you
have good drainage is to dig a hole in the
garden area that is 12 x 12 x 12 inches and
fill it with water. The suggested timing
for the water to drain out of the hole is all
over the board, depending on your source.
Some say it should drain completely
within 3 hours and others say that if it
drains about 2 inches an hour, it's good
drainage. The bottom line is that if there is
water standing in the hole 12 hours later,
you need to improve the drainage in this
garden before planting.

If you are really serious about checking
the drainage you can check with your local
Soil and Water Conservation service on
how to do a percolation test. But for most
gardeners, the above method works.

DRIFT

*A strategic grouping of plants
in the landscape.*

Much like the gracefully arching,
spreading winter snow drift over our
beloved gardens, some plants create a
similar appearance of movement. And
just like the snow, plants can drift, spilling
out, arching and covering the ground.
Many gardeners may liken it to a graceful
wave of flowers, such as with roses. If
you are gardening with plants that do not
have this drifting habit, the look of gentle

Hostas spilling over a garden path

movement in the garden can be created by installing individual plants grouped together in bands with curved instead of straight lines.

DROUGHT TOLERANT

A plant that can withstand longer periods of time without irrigation.

Dwarf citrus trees

DWARF

A smaller variety of a plant.

Dwarf varieties are much like their larger counterparts, just more petite in stature, making them ideal for containers and small garden spaces. Don't be fooled by the term dwarf, however, as it's a very relative term. Take the dwarf version of *Pinus mugo* or the mugo pine for instance; there are many dwarf cultivars available but you need to check out the mature size. One of the varieties *(P. mugo var. mughus)* grows to 8' tall. That's not what we consider dwarf!

ECOSYSTEM to
EXFOLIATING

ECOSYSTEM

A system consisting of a community of animals, plants and microorganisms, and the physical and chemical environment in which they interrelate.

EROSION

The moving or wearing down of material, such as soil and rock by wind, rain, and moving water.

Do you see that small rut in your garden bed and the pile of mulch in the lawn? That is an example of erosion. Barren hillsides are also very susceptible to erosion. Without the harnessing power of roots, soil can be easily swept away by water runoff, especially after heavy rain events. Fields that are bare, dry and deeply tilled can be eroded and top soil swept away by strong winds, forming giant dust clouds. Erosion is a bigger concern for farmers and at new construction sites; however, gardeners should be aware of it in their own landscape. Take steps to eliminate erosion when you see it in your landscape or it will just continue to get worse.

ESPALIER

Growing a plant in a single plane, often vertically against a wall or other support structure.

This ancient tradition of training fruiting trees to grow in such a way to maximize yield has been adapted to non-fruit-producing woody plants. The tree produces more fruit and benefits from the stored heat in the support wall, extending the growing season of the plant.

Traditionally a formal design element, the espalier design is equally at home in more relaxed settings, maximizing the limited space found in smaller, urban gardens and dressing up an otherwise unattractive, plain surface. It also provides a cooling effect for a building. It takes a little more time and effort to espalier a plant but the results are often quite attention-getting (if done right!).

EVERGREEN

Plants that keep their foliage year-round.

An evergreen eventually drops its needles or leaves (broadleaved evergreens) at some point throughout the year. Depending on the species, the plant

will typically have one distinct period in which all of the older foliage drops. A pine is an example of an evergreen that sheds its older needles. The various species of pine may keep their needles for three to five years, eventually shedding the older needles in the fall.

EXFOLIATING

When the bark of a tree or shrub has a peeling pattern.

To us humans, this term means to scrub or slough off the dead skin. In the world of plants, however, it's just a slight variation of this terminology. The term most commonly used is "exfoliating bark," which is kind of like taking off dead skin. Trees or shrubs that have exfoliating or peeling bark are usually quite attractive and it adds another dimension to the landscape value of the plant.

Betula nigra 'Cully' (Heritage® river birch)

FAIRY GARDEN
to FUNGUS

FAIRY GARDEN

A miniature garden in which the design includes dwarf or small plants and decorations to give the illusion that fairies occupy the garden.

Fairy gardens are whimsical and utilize plants and accessories that create the idea that this is a landscape in which tiny fairies hang out. Garden centers carry a line of small, dwarf plants that are suited for a garden of this nature. There are also lots of accessories such as houses, garden decorations, and other odds and ends that work well in fairy gardens (including items that you just might come across in your junk drawer!).

FAIRY RING

A naturally occurring ring or arc of mushrooms, or darkened rings of turf grass areas found in lawns.

Fairy rings are often attributed to a group of fungi that grows underground, feeding on decaying matter. As the fungus grows, it can sometimes result in a dead ring of turf grass surrounding a patch of green in the center. Or, you may see mushrooms growing in a ring or arc.

FASTIGIATE

A growth habit where the branches of the plant are erect and parallel to the trunk and central leader of the plant.

FERTILIZER

Any organic, inorganic, natural, or synthetic material added to the soil to provide nutrients for plant growth and production.

Plants need nutrients in order to grow and fertilizers are nutrients that can be added to the soil, based on a soil test recommendation, to meet this need. Fertilizers come in a variety of formulations including granular solids, water-soluble powders, liquids, and slow-release pellets; slow-release spikes and tablets are the most common. Most are spread on the soil or worked into the soil in granular form.

The fertilizer you select is up to you and your gardening philosophy. Fertilizers can be organic (of plant or animal origin), inorganic (being or composed of matter other than plant and animal; often of mineral origin), natural (occurring in nature) or synthetic (substances produced by chemical or biochemical means). Organic and naturally occurring fertilizers depend on microorganisms to break down and release nutrients; therefore, they take a little longer to be available to the plant. They also provide nutrients over a longer period of time. Inorganic fertilizers are readily available to the plants, but they can also be lost from the soil quickly, meaning you have to re-apply periodically. Synthetic fertilizers are man-made and specifically designed to provide certain nutrients to plants.

Whether you use organic, synthetic, liquid, granular, slow release, or any combination, following the product's instructions is critical. More of a good thing is not always better. Too much fertilizer can harm, burn, and even kill plants.

FIBROUS ROOTS

A profusely branched root system that occupies a large volume of soil around a plant's base.

Plants usually have either a taproot or a fibrous root system. Fibrous roots are profusely branched and occupy a large volume of soil around the plant's base. Plants such as peas, beans, tomatoes, and petunias have fibrous roots.

FLORICULTURE

The discipline of cultivating flowers or flowering plants, especially for ornamental purposes.

Floriculture typically involves growing bedding plants (including vegetables for the garden), flowering plants used for indoor decorations, cut flowers, and houseplants.

FLOWER

The showy reproductive part of a plant, made up of the petal, sepals, stamen and pistil.

Although a flower is usually the most visually appealing part of a plant, it has a greater function than just aesthetics. The flowers main function is to develop seeds. The flowering stage occurs after vegetative growth and before fruiting. Here are some basic parts of the flower and their function:

Petals – generally the colorful (though not always) part of a flower and attract pollinators.

Sepals – the often-green petal-like parts at the base of the flower and look like they are holding the petals together.

Stamen – the male part of a flower and is made up of the anthers and filaments. The anthers hold the pollen and are held up by a thread-like part known as the filament.

Pistil – the female part of the flower and has four parts. The stigma is the sticky surface at the very top of the pistil that accepts and traps and holds the pollen grain. The style is the tube-like structure that holds up the pistil and allows the pollen grain to grow down to reach the ovary. The ovary develops into fruit and contains the ovules, which develop into the seed.

FOLIAGE

The leaves of a plant.

Though most people go for plants with colorful flowers, many plants are prized for their fine foliage. Some plants have understated or nondescript flowers but their foliage is beautiful. For instance, many gardeners grow *Hostas* for their foliage alone. Shade gardeners relish the wonderful colors, textures and leaf shapes of coral bells and coleus. Incorporating plants that have unique foliage is a smart way to add season-long interest in your garden. Even if the flowers are spent, the foliage will take your garden well into late autumn and if evergreen, through the winter!

FOUNDATION PLANT

A plant that is typically used to hide or cover the foundation of a home, primarily older homes that have visible block foundations.

FRAGRANT

(See: Aromatic)

FRAGRANT GARDEN

A garden design that focuses primarily on plants that have good fragrance.

FREEZE THEN THAW

The occurrence of freezing temperatures followed by warmer temperatures, allowing thaw (changing from frozen to a liquid state) to occur.

We often use this term in gardening when referring to the result of the process on soil. During the winter months the soil freezes and thaws and the continual process of freezing and thawing can lead to heaving of plants.

FROST TOLERANT

Referring to plants that will withstand a frost and survive.

This term is generally used for herbaceous plants (soft green tissue) that are planted outside in the early spring, before temperatures warm up. They may not, however, withstand freezing temperatures. Therefore, if temperatures drop into the freezing range (upper to lower 20°F), even frost tolerant plants would have to be protected to survive. Plants in the frost tolerant group are those annuals such as snapdragons and pansies, and vegetables such as cabbage, broccoli, cauliflower, kale (photo), mustard, radish, turnip, and Brussels sprouts.

FRUIT

The ripened ovaries of the flowering part of the plant that contain the genetic material to start a new plant and can sometimes be eaten.

Botanically, that definition is correct, but it sure doesn't sound very tasty. The fact is, many fruits are encased in an edible, protective fleshy coating. The edible fruits are consumed by humans and animals, and the seeds of the fruit are distributed, dispersing the next generation of plants. Once the ovary is fertilized, the seeds develop and the ovary enlarges, forming the mature fruit.

The terms fruit and vegetable often get mixed and are confusing. Botanically speaking, a fruit always develops from a flower and is composed of at least one ripened ovary. A vegetable, botanically, is any other part of a plant that is eaten.

FUNGI/FUNGUS

The largest group of plant pathogens, often developing into colonies.

Fungi (plural of fungus) spread by spores that are carried by wind, water, or animals. They can enter into plant tissue either through natural openings such as flowers or through a wound caused by pruning or injury. They cause damage that eventually destroys plant tissues. Common fungus diseases include powdery mildew, rust, leaf spot, blight, root and crown rots, damping-off, smut, anthracnose, and vascular wilts.

Powdery mildew on squash

GARDEN TOOLS
to GYMNOSPERM

GARDEN TOOLS

Here are some of the many useful garden tools it's good to have at hand:

Garden knife: A metal knife with a blade about 6-7 inches in length, typically with a sharp edge and a serrated edge for cutting roots. Used for digging small holes, planting, and a variety of other garden chores.

Digging fork: A metal tool with strong pointed tines (usually 4) set on a long handle, for loosening and turning soil or compost.

Hoe: A tool with a thin piece of metal set at right angle to the handle, for weeding and for breaking up soil.

Rake: A long-handled metal tool with a broad head set with rows of "teeth," for gathering leaves or smoothing soil surface. Also, a flexible-headed tool, often of bamboo, for gathering leaves.

Scuffle hoe: A tool with a thin piece of metal that is angled to move back and forth across the surface of the soil to destroy small weed seedlings.

Shovel: A broad-panned metal tool with a rounded bottom edge set on a long handle, for scooping and moving loose materials, like soil, snow, etc.

Spade: Similar to a shovel but more suitable for digging with its flat bottom edge.

Trowel: A small hand tool with either a flat or curved blade, for digging and planting.

GAZEBO

Roofed garden structures, making them ideal for protection from the elements such as rain and snow – unlike arbors, which don't have roofs.

Gazebos are most often open on four sides, constructed of four corner posts and a solid roof. Some gazebos are temporary, made of plastic and metal poles and a canvas roof. Others are more formal and may be elegant in design with fluted columns and a roof peak topped with a cupola.

GENUS

A hierarchical level in plant naming, which comes below family and above species.

Think of genus as the first name of a plant's Latin or botanical name. A genus is a group of species that are related. The genus of a plant is always capitalized and in italics. The second word is the specific epithet which further describes the genus. It is also italicized, but lower case. Together these make up the species. Sometimes an example is the best definition: *Echinacea purpurea. Echinacea* is the genus and *Echinacea purpurea* is the species; it is in the aster family.

GEOTROPISM

Referring to the effect that gravity has on plants.

Shoots and stems grow up (negative geotropism or against gravity) and roots grow down (positive geotropism or with gravity). To see geotropism in action, lay a potted plant down on its side and watch the shoots eventually make a turn and grow up, towards the sky.

GERMINATION

The transformation process of a seed developing into a young plant.

For a seed to germinate, or transition in to a young plant, the conditions must be right, such as an elapsed cooling period or darkness followed by warming soil temperatures. Such conditions vary by type of seed.

In gardening we use the term germination period, which indicates how long after sowing (planting seeds) it will take before young plants emerge. Knowing the germination period allows gardeners, especially those who grow edibles, to calculate the best time to start seeds for the upcoming growing season.

GIRDLING

The removal of bark from around the circumference of a branch or trunk of a woody plant.

Sometimes, girdling is accidental or caused by vandalism; other times it is intentional. It can happen when you get too close to a tree with a lawn mower or weed eater. A branch or trunk can be "choked" due to wires, holiday lights, etc. Animals may also be the culprits: beavers girdle a tree trunk in the hope of felling the tree for use in dam building. Intentional girdling is a method used to thin a stand of trees, such as in a pine plantation. It's also used intentionally to encourage more fruit development on a fruit tree.

The section of stripped or removed bark consists of the phloem, cambium and sometimes may even go into the xylem, resulting in the decline and possible death of the plant. *Note:* in the case of girdling fruit trees to get more fruit, the layer just under the bark is carefully removed

for this technique. In this example, girdling is also known as ring barking.

GIRTH

The size of something measured around the middle.

In gardening terminology, girth is used to refer to the size of a tree around the trunk. This is expressed as DBH or diameter at breast height. DBH is measured at 4.5 feet from the ground.

GRAFT/GRAFTING

A type of propagation in which two separate plants are joined together to benefit from the ideal features of each to form a new plant.

One plant is selected for its root system and is commonly referred to as the "stock" or "root stock." Another plant is selected for its stems, leaves, fruit, and foliage and is called the "scion." Each possesses a quality or qualities that are desirable.

For the grafting to be successful, the vascular system of the stock and scion plants must be placed in contact with each other and the two vascular systems united. Both tissues must be kept alive until the graft has "taken," usually a period of a few weeks. The joint of the grafted plants is not as strong as naturally occurring joints in the trees.

GREEN MANURE

A term commonly used when a cover crop is tilled into the soil. (See: Cover Crop)

GREEN ROOF

A type of roof on a building that is completely or partially covered with plants.

Green roofs are appreciated for their good looks. But more than that, they are considered environmentally friendly, as they absorb rainwater, cool the building (helping to lower the air temperature in urban areas), and create a habitat for wildlife.

Green roofs require a special waterproof membrane over the structure as well as a special soil for the plants.

GREENHOUSE

A building or structure that provides protection from the outside elements for growing plants.

Often made of glass, greenhouses can be designed exclusively for growing plants or providing a warmer climate for non-hardy plants such  as tropicals. A greenhouse can be altered to create a second living space such as a dining area surrounded by plants.

At one end of the greenhouse spectrum are temperature controlled plant production buildings made of glass, complete with water, temperature controls and operating windows – which are usually more permanent structures. More conservative greenhouses are made of plastic (often called hoop or poly houses) and are not necessarily permanent and more easily moveable from location to location.

GREENING UP

Going from winter color to the emergence of bright, luscious, brand new spring plant color. (And more!)

These are the happy words uttered by lawn enthusiasts when their dormant lawn casts  off its dull, brown hue and slips on a pale green spring frock. Or it can refer to the greening-up of nutrient-deprived plants after a very welcome dose of fertilizer (a balanced diet does a plant and gardener good!), transforming the plants from tired and dull to green and vigorous.

In more recent years, greening-up can also mean becoming more environmentally aware and conscious. Greening-up is swapping out boiling rooftops for rooftop gardens, recycling, installing free-to-borrow bicycle stations in cities, and even eating local; capturing water runoff for use in the garden or directed to a rain garden; using composted garden and kitchen materials as soil amendment; and creating a bridge to sustainable landscaping – all ways that you can green-up your landscape and garden.

Liriope muscari (lilyturf)

GROUND COVER

Plant material which forms a dense mat, growing low to the ground.

Ground covers can be creeping, such as *Ajuga* (bugleweed), or upright, like *Liriope muscari* (lilyturf). They do best when planted *en masse* and help to conserve water, minimize weed seed germination (think alternative to mulch), and are excellent in erosion control. Some ground covers, such as the one above, are evergreen, adding winter interest to the garden or landscape.

GROW COVER

(See: Row Cover)

GYMNOSPERM

A vascular plant that produces seeds that are not protected in an ovary.

Conifers are gymnosperms, meaning they produce seeds that are not protected in an ovary. The seeds of pine trees, *Ginkgos* and cycads develop in open structures, such as on the surface of leaves, or on cones. You may hear them referred to as "naked seeds," even though the seeds are tucked within a cone and are not easily visible. Gymnosperm is in contrast to angiosperm, which has seeds enclosed within an ovary.

HABIT to
HYDRANGEAS

HABIT

The natural, mature shape or form of a plant.

When you are choosing a plant, you want to know that it is the right one for the right place or space. You need to know its habit and its mature height and width. Why pick a plant that will mature at a size or shape

that is beyond the boundaries within your landscape? It's like being a size 16 and trying to squish yourself into a size 12 pair of jeans! You can kinda/sorta make it work, but is it really worth the extra effort, time and money when you could simply buy a size 16 and have a perfect fit?

Often, the mature form of a plant is hard to discern from a juvenile plant in a container at the nursery. So look at plant tags, books, and reference materials to find a plant's mature height and width and its habit or growth form.

Types of Habits

Arching – The plant will grow up and away from the center line or trunk and then down towards the ground. An example is weeping cherries.

Upright – The plant will stand straight, compact and close to the center line, and have little to no downward leaning or turned branches. Shrubs used for hedging, windbreaks and privacy screens are upright.

Groundcover – The plants hug the ground closely in a tight mat, completely covering the soil when planted en masse. *Pachysandra*, *Ajuga*, ivy and *Vinca minor* are examples.

Spreading – The plants grow out and away from their center. They may branch out across the ground, like creeping jenny or other runner plants, or continually grow into an increased mass, like a large stand of bamboo. Spreading plants may form a dense ground cover. Care should be taken when planting spreading plants, for they may become invasive, crowd out other plants, or move beyond the desired planting area.

Sometimes growth habits are combined, such as upright arching, meaning the plant has an upright habit with branches that arch or grow away from the center of the plant.

HABITAT

The place in which we live; also, the places where animals and plants live.

When we talk of plants and animals we often refer to their natural habitat – a place where they thrive and survive best. Take plants out of their natural habitat (such as out of their hardiness zone) and a bit more care on the gardener's part is in order. Sometimes we can fib the habitat; for instance, generously watering please-keep-my-feet-wet plants that are installed in a slightly drier than desired area.

Habitat is also what we create as gardeners. We can select plants that offer little shelter or food for birds and insects, or we can select plants with the necessities of the wildlife in mind. It is quite rewarding to create a garden that is not only gorgeous and pleasing to our eyes, but is also a thriving habitat for birds, butterflies and beneficial insects.

HA-HA

An old English term for a sunk fence that has a ditch with one sloping side and one vertical side into which is built a retaining wall.

A ha-ha is used to create a barrier for animals while allowing an unbroken view of the landscape. Think of this as a ditch that you can't see in the distance, but only when you come upon it – hence the name. The idea was that you would have a barrier for the animals but not a fence or ugly structure that would block the view. Ha-ha!

HARDENING OFF

The act of preparing plants to go from warm greenhouse conditions to the harsh outdoor air, wind and sun exposure.

When plants are started in a greenhouse or indoors under warm conditions, they are tender. Green leaf tissue is soft and not ready to be exposed to direct sunlight, cold or wind. Hardening off is a gradual exposure to these conditions by placing them outdoors in a protected area and either

covering them with a row cover or placing them inside a cold frame.

Each day, expose the plants to the air and sunlight for a few hours at a time until eventually they are able to thrive or handle a full day of sun. You'll notice a difference in the leaf tissue when they go from appearing "thin-skinned" to "thick-skinned." You will hear the term acclimation used for this process as well. For instance, people moving from the North have to acclimate to the hot summers in the South.

HARDINESS/HARDY

The ability of a plant to withstand extreme weather conditions, most commonly cold or heat tolerance.

In general, a purchased plant should have a tag indicating a Plant Hardiness Zone number. The number correlates to a range of the coldest temperatures the plant can endure and still survive (i.e., overwinter or be cold hardy). (See zone maps, pp. 176, 177).

More recently, a parallel chart for heat tolerance was developed, called the AHS (American Horticultural Society) Heat Zone Map. This will indicate a plant's hardiness ability to survive the heat, sun, wind and periods of drought.

Of course, even though we're talking "green," everything is not always black and white, and in this case, hardiness does have a gray area. For instance, it is possible to take a perennial that is a Zone 7 plant and grow it in a Zone 6 locale, but instead of its coming back year after year, depending on the weather (how cold it gets that season), it may die off just like an annual. Another example

Average Annual Extreme Minimum Temperature 1976-2005		
Temp (F)	Zone	Temp (C)
-60 to -50	1	-51.1 to -45.6
-50 to -40	2	-45.6 to -40
-40 to -30	3	-40 to -34.4
-30 to -20	4	-34.4 to -28.9
-20 to -10	5	-28.9 to -23.3
-10 to 0	6	-23.3 to -17.8
0 to 10	7	-17.8 to -12.2
10 to 20	8	-12.2 to -6.7
20 to 30	9	-6.7 to -1.1
30 to 40	10	-1.1 to 4.4
40 to 50	11	4.4 to 10
50 to 60	12	10 to 15.6
60 to 70	13	15.6 to 21.1

is a re-blooming azalea, which is a Zone 6 plant. But it can be grown in a container in a Zone 5 climate and then strategically stored during the winter months in a protected spot or building and it will still thrive in the coming growing season.

HARDPAN

A layer in the soil that roots and water cannot penetrate.

Chances are, all gardeners have tried to dig through hardpan before, with futility. There are different reasons why a  hardpan forms; one of the most common causes is using a rototiller or similar type of machine too often. The tiller will keep the top layer of soil loose, but beneath the depth of the blades the continual tilling leads to compaction – and eventually a layer of soil that is impenetrable. This layer can be broken up by double digging (not an easy task, by the way!).

HARDSCAPE

Anything in the landscape that is not a living plant.

HARDWOOD

As in "hardwood cutting" – referring to the hard, mature (not soft and green) wood of a deciduous or evergreen plant.

Hardwood cuttings are one method used to propagate (reproduce) more plants. Wood is cut from plants when it is stiff and hard (such as during the fall or winter months). The opposite is softwood cuttings, which are produced during the growing season when wood cut from the plant is turgid (with swollen, moisture-filled tissues) but still pliable.

HEAD

As in the "head" of a tree.

This is the portion of the tree from the bottommost branches of the trunk upward. A "good" tree head has a straight central leader. This central leader means the trunk extends upward through the middle of the tree straight upward.

A less desirable tree head will have multiple leaders instead of just one. This is not the best choice, as these multiple leaders do not create as strong a tree and it can easily succumb to breakage due to heavy snow loads, wind and storm damage.

HEAVE/HEAVING

What happens in cold climates when plants are pushed up out of the ground due to the soil freezing and thawing continually over the winter months.

When plants heave, their roots are exposed to cold temperatures and drying winds and injury can occur. Plants that were just planted in the late summer and fall are especially sensitive to heaving because their roots haven't become established in the planting bed. A layer of mulch (approximately 6-8 inches) around the base of the plant will help to moderate soil temperatures and prevent heaving. Remove the mulch from the base of the plant in the spring.

HEELING IN

A temporary way to store a plant until it can be planted in its permanent location.

One would heel-in a plant in soil, a bed of mulch or sawdust, creating an atmosphere where the root mass is protected.

Plants can be bare root, balled & burlapped (B&B) or in a container. Trees and shrubs are placed in one of these mediums as a stop-gap measure.

Reasons to heel-in include:

- The ground is frozen.
- Soil is not prepared or amended.

- Or, if you are like us, you bought too many plants at the garden center and have to figure out where to put them! In the meantime, just find a temporary spot to heel them in.

HEIRLOOM PLANT

A plant that has been cultivated using the same methods for more than 50 years and whose seeds are passed down from generation to generation.

There really isn't an all-encompassing definition for heirloom plant. The Smithsonian Heirloom Gardens contain plants that were grown only before 1950.

Heirloom plants are open pollinated (no hybrids) and might have a better

flavor or fragrance than some of the varieties we have today. For instance, breeders have worked on tomatoes that withstand shipping and last longer on the grocery shelf. However, the tradeoff sometimes is hybrid plants with thick skin and lack of flavor. Heirloom plants usually survive for several generations through seed saving and the efforts of private individuals.

HERB

Botanically speaking, a seed-producing annual, perennial or biennial that doesn't produce woody stems and dies back at the end of the growing season.

In culinary terms, it is a plant with savory, aromatic or medicinal qualities.

HERBACEOUS

A plant that doesn't have woody tissue and dies back to the ground in the winter in colder climates.

We use this term broadly for a group of plants that includes bulbs, annuals, biennials and perennials. This term sometimes confuses gardeners because we put perennials in this group, yet there are some perennials that develop woody stems. However, they tend to die back to some degree or another, so they are still considered herbaceous.

HERBICIDE

A pesticide used to kill weeds or other plants.

Herbicide examples include:

- Bayer Crabgrass Killer
- Round-Up Extended Control
- Safer®Brand Fast Acting Weed and Grass Killer

HERBIVORE

An animal that feeds on plant material.

Herbivores can be a real menace in the garden as they don't distinguish from your good garden plants and plants in general! Therefore, herbivores such as deer, squirrels, and others can become a garden pest quickly.

HIGH TUNNEL

A crop-growing system that is structured somewhat between a greenhouse and row covers.

High tunnels are used to extend the fruit and vegetable growing season. They have greater capability than a row cover because you don't have to remove the cover to work on the crop; and they don't have the environmental controls (temperature, humidity, etc.) or the cost of a greenhouse.

They are similar to a greenhouse in that they are Quonset-shaped with supports made out of metal bows, which are covered in plastic. The high tunnel can be ventilated by manually rolling up the sides, allowing for air circulation. There is no heating system, though some have a portable heater that can be used to prevent freezing of plants in extreme low temperatures.

HIP

The fruit of a rose.

Most women don't want large hips, but when it comes to roses, sometimes the larger the better! Rose hips can be very ornamental and are usually orange or red, but can also be dark purple to black. These large, fleshy receptacles, which contain the seeds, have been used for jams, jellies, syrup, soup, beverages, pies and more. After the roses are pollinated, the hips begin to swell and turn color in late summer and fall for a beautiful display in the garden.

HONEYDEW

A sticky, sugary substance secreted by aphids and other plant sap-sucking insects.

As sucking insects feed, they produce large amount of this sugary liquid. Gardeners don't always see the actual culprit (aphids and soft scale the most common) but notice the honeydew. Cars, lawn furniture and other items under a plant that has a population of insects that produce honeydew may end up with the sticky substance on the surface. Sooty mold is a fungus that grows on honeydew and produces a blackened appearance to the surface, like it's covered with soot. Remove the honeydew as soon as you see it because the longer the sooty mold remains on the surface, the more difficult it is to remove.

HORTICULTURE

The art and science of cultivating plants.

Horticulture is the practice of growing flowers, fruit or vegetable plants, or ornamental

plants. Horticulture is one sub-sector under the umbrella of "Agriculture."

HOST

Something (plant, animal or other organism) that supports the growth of another plant, animal, organism, etc.

HYBRID

A new plant that is created from crossing two different plants.

This can happen in Mother Nature or intentionally in a lab by a hybridizer, a person who crossbreeds plants. The result is a plant with desirable

qualities of either or both parents.

HYDRANGEAS AND HOW TO PRUNE THEM

The number one question asked by gardeners is, "How do I prune my hydrangeas?" Unfortunately, the standard answer is, "it depends." The secret to knowing how to prune hydrangeas is to know what species you have. Hydrangeas are deciduous shrubs that have recently exploded in popularity as breeders are coming up with varieties that are fairly easy to grow.

When pruning hydrangeas, you have to determine if the blooms occur on "new" or "old" wood. In other words, do the flowers appear on growth from the current growing season or do they appear on the wood that was developed last year? If plants bloom on old wood

and you prune them in the spring, chances are you will cut off the flowers for the season. When in doubt on pruning, a good rule of thumb to follow is to prune right after blooming.

Here are the most common species grown in the landscape, with a description and the best time to prune.

Hydrangea anomala (Climbing)

An excellent clinging vine that grows to 60-80 feet in height. It needs a strong support, as the stems can get quite woody and heavy. The older stems have a beautiful, peeling, cinnamon-colored bark. The flowers bloom in early to mid-summer on old wood, so prune after blooming.

H. arborescens (Smooth)

This fast-growing shrub is native to the U.S. and gets around 3-5 feet tall and as wide. White flowers appear in the summer and last through most of the season on new wood. Therefore, you can prune them any time before they begin to grow in the spring. Cultivars of this species include 'Annabelle' and 'Grandiflora'.

H. macrophylla (Bigleaf)

These hydrangeas need more moisture or they don't make it in the garden. They can get around 3-6 feet tall and bloom for most of the summer. They bloom on old wood, and so should be pruned after flowering. The flowers are mopheads or lacecaps and can be pink or blue depending on the cultivar or the pH of the soil *(see: pH)*. Some cultivars will have blue flowers if the soil is acidic and pink flowers if the soil is alkaline.

H. paniculata (Panicle)

This species has flowers that are called panicles, or are more of a cone-like shape than the flat top of the above species. The flowers appear in mid-summer and can be around 6-8 inches long. The plant is cold-hardy and fast growing, reaching heights of about 20 feet. The flowers appear on new wood, so you can prune in the late winter or early spring, before the plant leafs out.

H. quercifolia (Oakleaf)

This slow-growing shrub can get to around 4-6 feet tall and wider, because it tends to sucker. The older stems exfoliate to reveal a beautiful, rich cinnamon brown bark, giving it a great winter appearance. The stems and buds are subject to winter injury if temperatures drop below -10F. A little winter protection or a protected area in the garden works best. The flowers are panicles and around 4-12 inches long and appear in July and last until September; they appear on old wood, so prune after flowering. The fall color of this shrub is also spectacular, with leaves of reds, orange-browns, bronze and purples.

INDETERMINATE
to IRRIGATION

INDETERMINATE

Referring to tomatoes, where growth of the plant is potentially limitless.
(See: Determinate)

 Indeterminate tomatoes can keep growing forever if you give them the right growing conditions! They keep putting on height as long as environmental conditions are conducive. That said, the continuous growth habit of the indeterminate tomatoes requires proper caging or staking to support the height and weight of the plant. These plants also require pruning in order to produce a good crop.

INFLORESCENCE

A cluster of flowers or the complete flower head of a plant, including the stems, stalks, bracts, and flowers.

INPUTS/OUTPUTS

In reference to what you put into or get out of gardening.

So many times we have been asked, *What can I plant that doesn't require a lot of work?* There are some pretty self-reliant plants but the truth is, as in life, the more you put into the garden, the more you get out. Inputs are fertilizer, soil amendments such as compost, water and of course, your time. Outputs are what your garden will give back to you: blooms, texture, color, beauty, delicious fresh fruits, veggies and herbs, enjoyment and a more beautiful home environment.

In green industry terms, input can refer to the number of liner or baby plants put into a container. So for instance, if you are creating a mixed container by planting four different annual plants in it, you are using four inputs.

INSECT

An animal in the class **Insecta.**

Assassin bug

All bugs are insects but not all insects are bugs! The term insect comes from a Latin word that means "cut in to." This refers to the body parts of an insect that are divided into three parts: the head, thorax, and abdomen. Insects breathe air and usually have three pairs of legs and usually two pairs of wings. People have a tendency to lump all insects together and call them bugs. Bugs are a sub group of insects that are considered true bugs and have piercing, sucking mouthparts. Additional insects include termites, grasshoppers, crickets, roaches, earwigs, lice, beetles, butterflies, moths, fleas, flies, gnats, mosquitoes, and bees.

INTEGRATED PEST MANAGEMENT

A combination of strategies used to manage garden pests.

If integrated pest management (IPM) were easily understood and easy to use, everyone would be doing it! However, it takes a little time and thought to incorporate IPM into your everyday work in the garden. IPM is a systematic approach to dealing with pests in the garden. It starts with best gardening practices, which include the right plant in the right location and good soil preparation. When a problem crops up, the next step in IPM is to determine the most effective and appropriate control for the situation.

It might include doing nothing, because the pest really isn't a huge problem to the plant or to you as a gardener. IPM options include cultural (irrigation, crop rotation, tilling, pest-resistant plants), mechanical (hand picking and removing of the pest, screens and barriers to prevent pest entry), biological options (letting the good bugs do their job) – as well as chemical options, with chemical options being the last choice. If you do choose to use chemicals, select the right product to target the pest and know the best time to apply.

INTERNODE

The space in between two plant nodes.

Think of nodes and internodes in terms of human anatomy: Nodes are like our wrists, elbows, ankles and knees, whereas the internodes are the area between the wrist and elbow or elbow and shoulder. It could also be like the area from the ankle to the knee or the knee to the hip.

Thus, the nodes are where the leaves, stems and shoots emerge from along a branch. Internode length can indicate plant growth rate. For instance, if the internode area is short, it can indicate a slow growing or dwarf plant selection or that the plant is not happy and not growing as it should. If the internode length is long, and it appears the plant is stretching, it might mean the plant is

in too much shade and it is not in the best landscape location for it to succeed. Or in the case of a houseplant, it means it needs more light and should be moved to a sunnier window location.

INTRODUCED

A plant that is not native and is brought into a region or area of the country and planted.

INVASIVE

A non-native species that is introduced to an ecosystem that causes or likely causes economic or environmental harm or harm to human health.

The dictionary uses words like invading or tending to invade, intrusive, or this statement: "characterized by or involving invasion; offensive." All of these terms might be used in gardening in reference to plants that have a tendency to be bullies. Plants that take over an area can be considered invasive, or some might call them aggressive. The government, of course, gives a much longer definition of an invasive species. A true invasive plant is something that gardeners should be aware of, be able to identify and remove, if possible, before it causes damage to an ecosystem. For more information on invasive species that might be found in your area, go to www.invasivespeciesinfo.gov.

IRRIGATION

The process of artificially applying water to a desired location.

There are many methods or tools used for irrigation: wells, ditches to pull water from a nearby stream or river, hoses and sprinklers, buckets and watering cans – and more advanced, controlled methods such as drip irrigation, soaker hoses and underground irrigation with pop-up sprinkler heads.

Soaker hoses have many, many tiny holes in which the water can pass through the surface of the hose very slowly. The soaker hose is placed close to the base of a plant, allowing water to be directed just to the plant, not the empty area surrounding it. Soaker hoses usually have a fine mist or slow drip, great for deep soaking.

Drip irrigation is mostly used in the nursery production and garden center trade. Suspended tubes fed by a main waterline deliver a continuous drip of water to a particular plant being grown in a pot. Drip irrigation alleviates hand watering and the slow drip of the water allows it to permeate the surface of the potted plant's soil and soak in deep to the roots. The water is directed to each plant so there is less excess waste.

Pop up-sprinkler heads from underground irrigation systems save the busy gardener from dragging heavy hoses around the yard. These are placed strategically around the landscape to water plants at specific times according to a controller set by the homeowner. One of the challenges that we see is that people tend to water lawns, flowerbeds and trees and shrub beds all the same. Make sure you water each group or type of plants according to their water requirements. To prevent the irrigation lines from freezing and breaking over the winter, the pipes or tubing must be completely drained or "blown out" each fall if they are installed below the frost line.

Soaker hoses, drip irrigation and underground irrigation systems are often set on timers, so watering occurs during ideal times of the day. But, it's a waste of money and resources to run the system when it is raining or when watering simply isn't needed, so they still need to be monitored to be most effective. It drives us crazy to see an irrigation system running in the middle of a rain storm!

LANDSCAPE to LOAM

LANDSCAPE

A term with many different meanings, all relating to the appearance of a garden.

When this term is used as a noun, it refers to a section or an expanse of scenery, usually extensive, that can be seen from a single viewpoint. In gardening, it is referring to your entire property, including the gardens, trees, shrubs, grass, hardscape (non-plant decorative materials) and more. When it's used as a verb, it refers to the act of creating a pleasing appearance to your property.

LANDSCAPE DESIGN

The development and decorative planting of gardens, yards, grounds, parks, and other types of areas.

A landscape design can be used to enhance the setting for your home. It should be the basis for developing your hardscapes and making plant selections. A good landscape design creates a beautiful aesthetic setting while solving challenges in your landscape, such as erosion, screening, or fixing general problem areas. Starting with a landscape design master plan, you can develop your landscape over time and not make the mistake of having to move something later on.

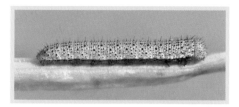

LARVA/LARVAL

The second stage of metamorphosis for insects (after egg).

An insect that undergoes complete metamorphosis has four stages to its life cycle. Those include egg, larva, pupa and adult. The larval stage for butterflies and moths is a caterpillar. The larval stage for beetles is a grub. Other examples of larvae (plural) are sawflies and maggots.

LATERAL BUD

A bud located at the sides of stems.

LATH HOUSE

An open-air garden structure that provides a shaded area for sheltering plants.

In general, a lath or shade house is a wooden structure that has shade cloth or wooden lath (spaced wood) as a roof, which blocks about 50% of the sun.

Lath houses hold plants that need a little TLC or protection from direct sunlight or other elements (like rain or wind) before being planted into the garden or shipped from the nursery. Freshly balled & burlapped, summer-dug plants in a wholesale nursery are often put into a shade or lath house until the tender plant tips harden off. Otherwise, branch tips wilt and will burn during the shipping process.

A lath house is useful when you purchase veggies or annuals in the spring, or you've started them from seed in your home. They need time to adjust from the greenhouse climate or warm house temperatures to  the colder, outdoor weather. Placing them for a few days in a lath house gives them time to harden off (acclimate) to the new environment while providing protection from the elements.

LAYERING

A way to propagate plants from a parent plant without having to take cuttings.

With layering you simply bend a thin branch to the ground and cover the center of the bent section with enough soil to secure the branch in place. If the branch is long enough, you can "plant" several sections of the branch in the soil. You will want to have a few leaves above ground between each "planted" section.

After a period of time, the planted section of the branch will develop roots. When the roots are sufficient, the branch can be removed from the parent plant and cut into sections, creating new plants with leaves and new roots identical to the parent plant. Because the branch used to propagate new plants is bent and buried once or multiple times in the soil, you will want to select a branch that is pliable so it won't snap or rip. This method works quite well with plants such as *Forsythia*, raspberries and blackberries, climbing rose and *Rhododendrons*.

LEACH

To drain away excess salts from the soil by the action of percolating liquid.

"Leaching the soil" is a term that refers to encouraging the salts to move out of the root zone. Salt buildup in the root zone can damage roots; therefore, leaching is a method used to remove salts from the soil or root system.

LEAD (IN SOIL)

An element that is occasionally found in your soil, which can lead to potential lead poisoning, particularly in children.

Most parents know about the dangers of lead poisoning and the effects it can have on children. Therefore, gardeners also need to be aware of the potential for lead poisoning that occurs as a result of gardening. Older homes that were built in the era when lead paints were used have a greater chance of lead appearing in the soil. Contamination may occur when paint chips from the house mix with the soil. Urban areas where there is a high rate of auto emissions may also have high rates of lead in the soil. Studies have shown that the highest concentrations of lead in soil occur around building foundations and within a few feet of busy streets.

A soil test that specifically tests for lead will indicate if there are any concerns to planting a garden in that particular area. Removing the soil and replacing with new can be expensive and a lot of work; therefore, design a raised bed garden and bring in new soil. Plants don't typically take up lead in the soil, however, leafy vegetables (lettuce, spinach, etc.) and root crops (carrots, potatoes, etc.) may have lead on the surface from contact with soil. Children playing in the soil are at greater risk for lead poisoning.

LEADER

The main, center branch of a tree; the trunk, which gradually narrows as you go higher into the tree.

All other side branches are attached to and grow outward from the central leader. Well, maybe not all the time, but at least this is what we shoot for when pruning landscape trees. Sometimes, a tree will have a couple of branches that compete for that main central leader spot. If one is not pruned out when the plant is young, then neither branch wins and the tree ends up with no true central leader – or what is called a double leader in the tree head.

A central leader is a sign of plant quality. It is most desirable to purchase a tree with a straight central leader, as it will have a nicer shape as it grows and matures. More importantly, it will have a better chance of handling snow and ice loads without breakage. Understandably, the less expensive plant with two leaders may be more appealing in the short term, but when it splits during a storm, landing on your house or across your car, you'll be wishing you'd have invested a few extra dollars on a quality plant with a strong central leader.

Vanderwolf's pyramidal pine

LEAF/LEAVES

The part of the plant whose main function is producing food for the plant; also known as foliage.
(See: Plant: Parts of the Plant)

LEAF HUMUS/LEAF MOLD

Decaying leaves, used as an organic matter to improve the soil.

Humus is the long lasting, stable remnant of organic matter. Leaf humus is the same, but derived from leaves. After leaves break down or decay, they make wonderful organic matter to add to the soil in order to improve soil structure. Leaf humus is great! Left alone in the woodland areas, leaves eventually break down, but you can make leaf humus for your garden by chopping the leaves into smaller pieces (running over them with a lawn mower) and letting them decay naturally. Chopping them speeds the process.

LEAF MARGINS

(See: Margin and page 88)

LEAF OUT/BUD BREAK

When the buds "break open" after a dormant period.

Often following a dormant period after a continuously colder season (winter, for example), the buds of plants, trees and vines break open and start growing. They reveal flowers, leaves, or branches, and new growth begins when consistently warmer weather returns in the spring.

LEAF PATTERN

The arrangement of the leaves on a plant.

The four most common leaf arrangements that can be found on plants are alternate, opposite, subopposite, and whorled. The way the leaves are arranged helps to classify a plant into the right category *(see: Taxonomy)* and helps to identify the plant in question. Alternate is the most generally

Alternate leaf arrangement on chestnut

referred-to leaf arrangement on plants. Alternate leaves are arranged on the stem in alternating fashion, while opposite leaves are arranged directly across from each other. Subopposite leaves are arranged so that they aren't quite opposite and aren't quite alternate but rather just slightly off from being across from each other, and whorled is when there are three or more leaves attached to the stem at the same location.

LEAF SCORCH

A plant disease resulting in a burned or scorched appearance of the leaf.

Leaf scorch can appear as a burned look along the margin (or edges) of the leaf or as leaf spots. Lack of water getting to the leaves tends to be one of the main causes.

LEAN

(See: Soil)

LEGGY

What we call a plant that gets out of control and grows tall and straggly.

This typically happens to plants that like full sun but are planted in the shade or you have a plant that prefers a lot of light in a darker room in the house. They end up stretching for light and becoming leggy or spindly.

LENTICEL

Cells on the surface of a stem on a plant that allow the exchange of gases between the plant and the outside.

Lenticels are sometimes prominent and very visible on some stems, while at other times, are very subtle and difficult to see. We use the appearance of lenticels on some plants to help us with identification.

LINER PLANT

Small-size plants that are sold to a wholesale nursery or greenhouse who will grow them on to a saleable size.

A liner plant is a tree, shrub, perennial, etc., that has been reproduced by varying methods of propagation. In turn, it will be sold to another wholesale greenhouse or nursery who will generally re-pot or re-plant the item so it can grow to a larger size, which can be sold to the consumer.

LOAM

A type of extremely fertile and desirable soil which is almost equal parts sand, silt, and clay.

A loamy soil is the trifecta of soil and one secret to gardening success. Understanding the soil composition of your garden or landscape enables you to amend your soil as needed, as well as select plants best suited for your garden's soil.

Loamy soil tends to hold water well without saturating roots, provides for maximum air circulation around the roots and has a capacity to hold nutrients. A loamy soil is so much easier to work in and dig (as opposed to those of us who have heavy clay soil and have to use a jackhammer to plant a tree!).

Soils that are heavier with clay or lighter with sand can, over time, be improved and become healthier and more desirable by adding and incorporating organic matter. (*See: Soil* and *Amendments*)

Liriodendron tulipifera (tulip poplar) leaf margin (and in bloom!)

MACRONUTRIENTS
to MYCORRHIZA

MACRONUTRIENTS

The main nutrients that are needed by plants in relatively large amounts.
(See: Nutrients)

These are divided into primary and secondary macronutrients. These essential primary nutrients are: nitrogen (for foliage growth), phosphorus (for root growth) and potassium (required for numerous plant growth processes). The secondary nutrients are calcium, magnesium and sulfur.

MANURE

Animal dung.

We didn't really have to give you the definition of manure did we? Since most people know what manure is, how about learning how it relates to gardening?

Composted manures are excellent sources of organic matter for a garden. Never use fresh manure, as this is high in nitrogen and can burn plants. In addition, fresh manure may have a higher potential of transmitting human pathogens such as *E. coli* and should not be used on edible crops. Allow manure to sit in a pile and break down for about a year before using. Manures can also be used as a fertilizer. Composted manures typically have lower nutrient levels and are slower to break down.

MARGIN

The area along the edge of a leaf blade.

We use the margins of a leaf to help identify plants. Leaf margins can be lobed, toothed, smooth, wavy, serrated, crenate, undulate, spinose, and more.

LEAF MARGINS

Lobed: with rounded edges and indentations that are at least ¼-inch from the margin to the primary vein

Serrate: toothed with the teeth pointing towards the tip of the leaf

Double serrate: toothed with larger teeth followed by smaller teeth in between

Crenate: teeth are rounded off

Undulate: wavy

Entire: smooth, no teeth, indentations or lobes

Dentate: outward pointing teeth all the way around the leaf

MATURE

A fully grown plant that has reached its maximum potential size.

It is critically important to check the mature size of a plant before you purchase to be sure it is well suited for the planned site in the landscape. It is far easier to install a plant in an area where it can grow to its full size than spend years trying to keep its size in check through pruning or having to remove and replace it with something smaller.

So, keep in mind that age also does not necessary determine a plant's maturity. Did you know that English ivy cannot reach maturity until it grows vertically? Only when English ivy climbs can it evolve from its juvenile state to its mature state and have the ability to flower and produce fruit. English ivy may remain in a juvenile state indefinitely when maintained as a ground cover. Plants really are pretty amazing, aren't they?

METAMORPHOSIS

A change in form from one state to the next in the life of an organism such as an insect.

Some species of insects have complete metamorphosis in which the life cycle includes the egg, larvae, pupa, and adult stage. Others have incomplete metamorphosis in which the change is very gradual and there is no pupal stage.

Complete metamorphosis of black cutworm

Incomplete metamorphosis of hairy chinch bug

MICROCLIMATE

An area with a little different climate from that of the region around it.

As an example, the temperature in an urban city is usually warmer than that of a rural countryside. On a smaller scale, everyone has some type of microclimate in their yard. The south side of your house is usually warmer than the north side, where the sun might not reach. A woodland area is going to be a little bit cooler than the middle of the yard that is in direct sun. Gardeners can take advantage of microclimates to grow plants that might need a little protection. Or they can create microclimates in the landscape by planting evergreens in order to block the wind or to cool things down a little with a shade tree.

MICRONUTRIENTS

Mineral nutrients needed by plants in smaller amounts than macronutrients, but also important. (See: Nutrients)

MONOECIOUS

Plants that house both male and female reproductive parts on the same plant.

The opposite of dioecious.

The Hemlock tree is an example of monoecious

MOUND

A growth habit where the branches are close together, reaching up and out to form a tight, compact half-circle shape.

Think of a ball buried halfway in the ground.

MULCH

Any material used to cover the soil of a garden bed or around a tree planting.

Mulch can vary from shredded bark to pine straw, gravel or pea stone. Mulch is a great gift to gardeners as not only does it finish off a garden, making it look neat and tidy, but it also conserves water, reduces the germination of weed seeds, and when organic matter is used, can enhance the quality of the soil. The organic mulch options – those derived from once live material such as leaves, needles, compost and bark – will gradually break down and add desired amendments to the soil.

Do note that over time mulch can become compact and tight, and act much like a duck's feathers, causing water to bead and run off rather than soaking into the garden. It is best to softly fluff or loosen the mulch at least once a year (if not more often) before watering. In addition, don't over-mulch plants. The recommendation is around two to four inches of mulch, keeping it away from the crown of the plants. And for heaven's sake, don't "volcano mulch."

Over-mulching can occur over time if you are using organic mulch such as hardwood bark. Each year gardeners like to freshen up the mulch and add more to make it look good. However, the mulch breaks down slowly and you may not need the same amount of mulch each year. Save yourself some money and add just a little bit of new mulch on top of the bed each season.

MYCORRHIZA

A fungus that helps plants absorb water and essential nutrients.

There is a lot going on below the surface of your garden. Colonizing within the roots of your plants is a fungus that helps the plants absorb water and essential nutrients. In return, the host plant provides the fungus with carbohydrates. It's a win-win situation for both plant and fungus!

Straw mulch in the potato patch

Schizachyrium scoparium 'MinnBlueA' (Blue Heaven™ little bluestem)

NATIVAR to NUTRIENTS

NATIVAR

A cultivar or hybrid of a native plant.

Nativars' parent plants are native to the area and so are believed to be more beneficial to the landscape and wildlife than other plant cultivars. Nativars are selected to exhibit the more attractive plant qualities of the native plants such as bigger blooms, larger leaves, dwarf size or other gardener-desired qualities, while still remaining closely related to the native plant.

There is a lively debate as to the validity of the assumption that nativars are an acceptable substitute to native plants. Some opponents contend that nativars may not be as recognizable and accepted by the pollinators as their true native counterparts. Others contend that any plant that is closely related to the native species should be used without exception over alien, cultivated species.

Echinacea 'Cheyenne Spirit'
(Cheyenne Spirit coneflower)

NATIVE PLANTS

A plant that occurs naturally in a particular region, ecosystem, or habitat without human intervention.

The generally accepted time frame for plants to be considered native is that the plants were present at the time Europeans arrived in North America.

NATURALIZE

When a plant fully acclimates to its new environment, giving the appearance of having grown there on its own.

When plants naturalize, it means they like where they are and have set up their household. They are usually introduced to an area of the landscape and then spread to appear as if they have been there forever. The design is more free flowing rather than formalized, such as bulbs scattered haphazardly through a woodland garden.

NECROSIS

The death of cells or tissues in a living organism.

Necrosis comes from the Greek term death or the stage of dying. In plants, necrosis can be seen on all plant parts including leaves, stems, roots, flowers, and fruit. It may appear as wilting, brown, dried-up leaves and branches or as dead spots on the root system. Necrosis is not a disease but may be a symptom of a disease or an insect. Necrosis can be caused by a host of issues: mineral-deficient soil, inadequate water, or damage to

the vascular plant tissue by pests.

NECTAR

The sweet, irresistible, life-sustaining liquid produced by plants to draw in pollinators like bees, hummingbirds and moths.

Nectar is produced in glands called "nectaries" within flowers. By luring in bees and other pollinators, plants ensure their genetic line continues by becoming pollinated by the feasting winged visitors that pass from one plant to another of the same species.

NEMATODE

A microscopic, eel-like roundworm.

Nematodes can live and feed in plant parts, causing damage. The most troublesome ones are those that live in plant roots, though there are foliar nematodes that can cause damage as well.

NEUTRAL

Referring to soils that have a pH of 7. (See: pH)

NIDUS

A nest or breeding place, or a place in an animal or plant where bacteria, insects, seeds, and other organisms breed and multiply (and a great term to impress your gardening friends).

In entomological terms, a nidus is a place for insects to lay their eggs.

NITROGEN

One of the major nutrients that plants require in order to form chlorophyll, the green pigment responsible for photosynthesis. (See: Nutrients)

Nitrogen helps plants with foliage growth, leading to increased seed and fruit production, as well as quality leaves. Nitrogen quickly moves through the soil and is not available for long periods of time. On the analysis of the nutrients in a bag of fertilizer, the first number is N, or percent nitrogen. If the label indicates that the fertilizer has an analysis of 5-10-10, it means that 5 percent of the total bag weight is nitrogen.

NODE

The part of the stem where a leaf appears or where a bud or side-shoot emerges.
(See: Internode)

It is often swollen and may look like a joint or bend in the stem.

N-P-K

An abbreviation for three primary macronutrients: Nitrogen, Phosphorus and Potassium.

NURSERY

A production center in which plants are grown in preparation for sale.

Nurseries can produce liners (baby plants), which they sell to another grower. Other nurseries propagate plants themselves or buy a liner and grow it on to a saleable size (a larger size more commonly sold at retail). Some nurseries are more like retail shops in which plants are brought in, cared for, and marketed to gardeners so the actual growing is more a matter of just maintaining the plant for a quick sale. Nurseries may also sell soil, mulch, soil amendments, garden accessories, and other garden related items. Nurseries, in particular those who grow and sell their own plants to the general public, can be used interchangeably with a retail garden center.

NUT/NUTLET

A fruit with an ovary that has dried to a hard protective coating. Within the ovary-turned-shell is one seed or nut.

The outer covering of the chestnut fruit

NUTRIENTS

The base mineral components a plant needs to survive.

We fertilize plants, we don't FEED them – they make their own food through the process known as photosynthesis. Plants require nutrients, macronutrients as well as micronutrients. Macronutrients are those that are required in generally higher levels and include nitrogen (N), phosphorus (P) and potassium (K); these are the primary macronutrients. Secondary macronutrients include calcium (Ca), magnesium (Mg), and sulfur (S). Micronutrients are required in lower amounts and include boron (B), copper (Cu), iron (Fe), chloride (Cl), manganese (Mn), molybdenum (Mo) and zinc (Zn).

People outside of Ohio tell us that buckeyes are "worthless nuts!"

OPEN-POLLINATED to OVERWINTER

OPEN-POLLINATED

Pollination of a plant by wind, birds, insects, humans or other natural mechanisms. (See: Heirloom Plant)

Plants that result from open pollination can be quite diverse since the fertilization process in not controlled in a laboratory setting. These plants adjust to their environment, such as the growing conditions, which means new plants that are more adapted to their location; i.e., they are already Mother Nature tested. It's the survival of the fittest plant offspring in action! Genetically speaking, open pollination creates broader genetic variations in plants.

OPPOSITE/ALTERNATE

The order in which leaves attach to a stem. (See: Leaf Pattern)

You may not think knowing if a plant has alternate or opposite leaves is important until the day you come across a

plant you do not recognize and you want to describe it to someone in the know. When keying out a plant, identifying the manner in which a leaf attaches to the stem in relation to the other leaves is very important. Do the leaves attach to the stem opposite to each other or are they alternating?

ORGANIC MATTER

Something that is derived from or has characteristics of living things.

Organic matter is the part of the soil that consists of plant or animal tissue in various stages of decomposition. Organic matter provides great benefits to the soil and consequently plant growth. It improves soil structure or tilth, improves drainage in clay soils and increases water-holding capacity in sandy soils provides a source of slow release nutrients, reduces wind and water erosion, and promotes the growth of earthworms and other beneficial soil organisms.

ORNAMENTAL

A plant that has purely decorative value in the garden.

OUTPUTS

(See: Inputs/Outputs)

OVERGROWN

When a plant has outgrown the space for which it was selected.

Having overgrown plants is a sure sign you have either been away from your garden for far too long (and haven't done proper

pruning and maintenance) or picked a plant that was bound to outgrow the area for which it was originally intended.

Overgrown plants become too large for their surroundings and crowd out other plants, block walkways, ruin the aesthetics of a garden or outgrow their containers. To avoid this situation, select the right plant for the right place from the get-go and take care to prune and thin the plants you do choose in a timely fashion, and as recommended.

OVERSEED

*Usually referring to lawn care –
to scatter seed over thin places in
a lawn to thicken the turf.*

OVERWINTER

The process of a plant remaining alive over the winter.

A gardener wants to make sure that when they purchase a plant it's going to live through the winter in their landscape. In northern climates it's likely that the plant will overwinter in the dormant stage and then come out in the spring, ready to grow for the season.

PANICLE to PUBESCENT

PANICLE

The growth or habit of a flower where there is a branched raceme, or stem, in which each branch off of the main stem branches again.

A panicle structure creates thick, dense flower heads such as those of *Astilbe* (left photo) or *Hydrangea* (photo below).

PARASITE

An organism that lives in or on another organism and relies on it for food or shelter.

In the garden, parasites can be good or bad, depending on the species. For instance, there is a small parasitic wasp called *Cotesia congregatus* that lays its eggs on the back of the tomato hornworm. When the eggs hatch, the larvae feed on the inside of this very large caterpillar, eventually killing it. Look for the white

cocoons protruding from the back of the hornworm and let them do their job!

Another example of a parasite that causes harm to its host plants is dodder. Dodder looks like someone was trying to untangle a huge mess of fishing twine and threw it on top of a plant in frustration.

Dodder

The orange-to-yellow thread-like stems can be thin or somewhat stout, and have no leaves. The seedlings germinate in the ground and quickly attach to a suitable host within a few days or they die. It settles in on the plant and twines itself around the stems and loses its connection with the ground. It's totally dependent on the host to live.

PARASITOID

An insect that completes its larval development within the body of another insect, eventually killing it.
(See also: Parasite)

Parasitoids fall under the category of beneficial insects as they tend to feed on the bad guys.

PATHOGEN (PLANT)

An agent that causes diseases in plants.

Plant pathogens can be a fungus, bacteria, virus, or other microorganism. Most pathogens are host specific, which means that they only attack certain plants. For instance, the pathogen that causes black rot on grapes (photo) is a different pathogen than the one that causes black spot on roses.

PEAT

An organic material comprised primarily of partially decomposed plant material.

Peat is found naturally in wetlands, bogs and other damp areas. While a natural result of decomposing plant material, peat is not considered a renewable resource

due to the extreme length of time it takes to create peat.

Peat is used as a soil amendment. Since it is a sterile substance, it is ideal for seed starting as it helps reduce disease. A gardening shift is taking place, questioning whether peat should be used in the garden to improve the structure and organic makeup of the soil. Since peat is widely considered a non-renewable resource, many gardeners are using compost as an alternate to amend their soil. If you choose to incorporate peat into your garden soil, be certain to work it in well. Peat left on the surface dries easily and absorbs water from the soil, drying out the garden.

PEAT POTS

Containers made out of peat, which can be placed directly in the ground.

A seed can be started and grown in a peat pot and then directly planted in the soil without disturbing the plant. Make sure that you remove the top portion of the peat pot that might end up sticking out of the soil. Air moving over the top of the pot that sticks out of the ground causes the water to wick or move up the pot and dries the root system out faster. In addition, if the pot is relatively new and intact (hasn't started to break down), you might want to slit and tear the outside a little bit in order to allow the roots to have good contact with the soil sooner.

PENDULOUS

A descriptive term often used for flowers or plant growth habit where there is a weeping-type effect.

Just like the pendulum of a clock that hangs down and sways from side to side, so do pendulous flowers and plant branches. Weeping willows and weeping cherry trees are examples of a pendulous growth habit for a tree.

Flowers from a fuchsia plant

PERCOLATION TEST

A test used to determine how fast water moves through the soil.
(See: Drainage)

PERENNIAL

A plant that lives for more than one year but may die back in the winter and re-emerge the following spring from its crown or root system.

As with all plants, there are advantages and disadvantages to perennials. The advantages in using perennials in your flowerbed are that they come back year after year, the overall flowerbed or border changes throughout the season, you can divide and share the wealth, and they

come in many varieties, shapes, colors and sizes. The disadvantages are that some can be more costly than annuals (but you only plant them

Alchemilla mollis (lady's mantle)

once, hopefully), most of them have a shorter bloom period than annuals, and... they come in many varieties, shapes, colors and sizes. How can this last one be an advantage and a disadvantage? Because there are so many perennials and cultivars on the market today, it can be overwhelming when it comes to designing a pleasing flowerbed that blooms all season. However, put your design on paper and take a look at bloom times so that you can figure out the gaps and then fill in.

Many perennials can be divided to produce plants identical to the parent plant. Be certain to research the best time to dig and divide your perennials (creating multiple baby plants out of one large one) and if division is advisable and even possible. Some perennials, such as *Baptisia*, do not like to be disturbed once they are established.

PERGOLA

A free-standing structure in the garden with posts and a ceiling made of slatted wood. Unlike arbors, pergolas are generally larger in size and designed to cover or shade an area.

It may sound like we are splitting hairs here, but there is a difference between pergolas and arbors. Think of a pergola as a room within the garden, with or without vining plants and an arbor as the hallway or structure through which we pass to enter different areas within the garden.

Pergolas and gazebos are very similar. A pergola tends to be a structure that has open sides, provides shade and has unobstructed views.

PERLITE

A volcanic glass that is formed by the hydration of obsidian. It is a component of potting soil mixes.

Perlite is added to heavy, tightly bound soils to help open up the soil so it can accept more air and water. By loosening the soil, it allows the roots to better grow and take up water and nutrients, and air to circulate more freely. It is a lightweight, inexpensive gift to gardeners that is frequently used in container soil mixes.

PERMACULTURE

A term coined by Australians Bill Mollison and David Holmgren in 1978 for a branch or culture of gardening that breaks down the barrier between yard, home, woods and fields and strives to create landscapes that are intertwined and based on natural environments.

A permaculture landscape includes the home, yard, tree line and forest – all designed in relationship to each other, as it would be in nature, to create the most efficient, self-sustaining ecosystem possible. Trees that provide nuts and fruits are selected over purely ornamental varieties and native plants are always selected over hybrid plants. Plants are also grouped in zones as they would appear naturally, such as a large canopy tree, understory tree and groundcovers and shrubs that share the same soil condition and water requirements that naturally support each other. Where we often "fool" hardiness zones and water and soil requirements by supplementing our gardens, true permaculture landscapes do not require such measures.

PEST RESISTANT/ PEST TOLERANT

Terms used to describe a plant's ability to withstand pest damage.

A plant that is resistant won't be affected by a specific insect or disease. The resistance can be physical (fuzzy or waxy leaf surfaces) or chemical (enzymes that kill pathogens) characteristics or growth patterns (able to block off diseased tissue).

A plant that is tolerant may be affected by the specific insect or disease but won't be impacted to the point of plant decline or eventually death. A tolerant plant can still grow and maintain an acceptable appearance or produce a good crop.

PESTICIDE

"-cide" is a suffix that means "a killer of." Therefore, a pesticide kills pests.

Pests in the garden and landscape can cause harm to plants – insects, diseases, rodents, slugs, bacteria, fungi, weeds, and more. It's important to use the right pesticide on the pest that's causing problems. For instance, an insecticide won't kill slugs and snails, but a molluscicide will. Before a pesticide is used, make sure to identify the pest in question and determine if the timing is appropriate to use a pesticide. Then, select the right pesticide and follow label directions carefully.

TYPES OF PESTICIDES

Algicides – for algae

Fungicide – for fungi

Herbicide – for weeds

Insecticide – for insects

Miticide – for mites

Molluscicide – for mollusks (snails, slugs)

Rodenticide – for rodents

PETALS

(See: Flower)

PETIOLE

The stalk that attaches the leaf blade to the stem of the plant.

Not all leaves have petioles. Some leaf blades are directly connected to the stem or may even wrap around the stem.

pH

In soil, the degree of its acidity or alkalinity – measured in pH units.

The key ingredient for all successful gardens lies in the soil. The soil's pH level dictates which plants will do best. While the pH scale ranges from 0 to 14, the best soil pH for most plants is between 6.0 and 6.8.

Acidic soils have a pH range from 4 (very acidic) to 7, and alkaline soils have levels above 7.0 pH. Each unit change in pH levels (i.e., from 5 to 6) represents a 10-fold increase in the amount of acidity or alkalinity.

For a plant to thrive, nutrients in the soil need to be available for the plant to use, and nutrients need to have been dissolved in the soil. The majority of required nutrients are more available to a plant when the pH is in the middle of the range (6 to 7). Acid-loving plants (e.g., azaleas, rhododendrons, blueberries, etc.) prefer soils that are lower in pH (around 5 to 6).

Sometimes nutrients are unavailable to plants or become "locked" in the soil, preventing plant uptake. If the pH is in the extreme range – for instance, a 10 – the nutrients may still be in the soil, but are not in a form that is available to the plant. When the acidic level of the soil drastically rises, aluminum (a material that is not used by plants) is released into the soil, poisoning most plants.

How to determine the pH of your soil. This is done with a soil test. First, consult your local Cooperative Extension office for soil testing locations in your area, as well as the proper methods for soil testing. The results will be as good as the sample provided. Garden centers sometimes test soil or sell home test kits. Keep in mind that the results from these are not as reliable as those from a laboratory. However, they may be sufficient for the casual gardener.

It is good to check your soil every year in case it needs amending. It is especially important to test a new landscape area so you can either amend the soil and/or purchase plants that will do well in the established pH range. While the pH level of the soil can be altered, doing so is time-consuming and is best done in small areas, with the intention to raise or lower the pH of the soil a small amount.

pH SCALE

(See: pH)

PHLOEM

The part of a plant's vascular system responsible for transporting sugars to the roots and throughout the plant.

 These sugars are manufactured in the leaves through the process of photosynthesis. The phloem is located to the outside of the cambium layer in a tree and is just beneath the bark. If a lawn mower or weed eater, for instance, damages the bark of the tree, it usually cuts into the phloem, preventing sugars from getting down to the roots. Tree decline and possibly death can result if the damage is severe enough.

PHOSPHOROUS

A macronutrient needed for plant shoot and root growth. (See: Nutrients)

Phosphorus is essential for cell division in the plant. Phosphorous moves slowly through clay soils and therefore, a soil test should be completed before adding additional phosphorous to the soil. On the analysis of a fertilizer bag, the middle number is P, or percent phosphorous. If the label indicates that the fertilizer has an analysis of 5-10-10, it means that 10 percent of the total bag weight is phosphorus.

PHOTOSYNTHESIS

The process wherein plants convert light energy into food.

Photosynthesis is the process used by plants in which the leaves use light energy to convert carbon dioxide and water into sugars and oxygen.

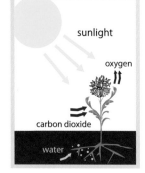

Sugars are used by the plants and oxygen is released.

PICOTEE

A flower that has one main color with a margin of another color.

PINCHING

A type of pruning method in which you use your fingers to remove the soft herbaceous tissue, usually the growth tips, to encourage branching of the stems.

PISTIL

(See: Flower)

PLANT: PARTS OF THE PLANT

Roots: Roots serve as anchors, keeping the plant in the soil and from falling over; they also absorb water and minerals from the soil and serve as a storage organ for food.

Stems: The primary function of a stem is to support the plant. The stem also conducts water and nutrients from the roots and food (after photosynthesis) to other parts of the plant. Stems can be woody like a tree or shrub or they can be herbaceous with soft green tissue.

Leaves: Leaves are the food-making factory of the plant, capturing sunlight and making food for the plant through the process of photosynthesis.

Flowers: Flowers serve as the reproductive organ of the plant and contains pollen and ovules (tiny eggs). The ovule develops into the fruit.

Fruit: Fruit is the covering for the seeds and can be fleshy like an apple or hard like a walnut.

Seed: Seeds form in the fruit and ensure that the species continues to survive, producing a new plant.

PLANT PATHOLOGY

The study of plant diseases.

PLANTING BED

An area of ground prepared for growing plants.

How a bed is prepared varies on the type of gardening you plan to do as well as your existing soil. A planting bed may be well defined with crisp edges, a brick border, mulch line – or raised with the use of timbers, stones or mounded soil. Other beds may be at grade level and simply be turned, amended and prepared for plants, with the end result being a garden that blends naturally into the surrounding landscape.

POD

A dry fruit (pericarp) that splits at maturity and is composed of one or more carpels (where the seeds develop).

Honeylocust seed pod

POLLARDING

A pruning technique in which you remove the upper branches of a tree back to its trunk in order to encourage a dense growth of foliage close to the trunk.

For centuries, this was a common practice in Great Britain and Europe and you will still see it in some cities as a way to maintain trees at a certain height. Pollarding was used to encourage new growth each year in order to supply new wood for various purposes such as for fuel, stored as winter fodder for stock, as well as used for making baskets.

Pollarding is different from topping trees. When pollarding is done the right way, the branches cut are only one or two years old. When trees are topped, the branches cut are usually large and don't have the tendency to naturally seal off the wound. The remaining branch decays, leading to a weakened branch structure for supporting any new growth.

POLLEN

A small, coarse, powder encased in a protective coating that contains the sperm or the male DNA of plants.

While pollen may cause allergies to flare up and settle into a fine dusting on our tables and blinds, despite its annoyances, it is the stuff of plant life. Pollen is carried by wind and wing, primarily. When it comes into contact with a compatible female stigma or cone, it sets in motion the next generation of plants.

POLLINATION/ POLLINATOR

The process of pollen being transferred from the stamens (male) to the stigma (female) to accomplish fertilization. The pollinator is the vehicle that moves the pollen.

It is believed that 80 percent of plant fertilization is dependent on pollinators.

Halictid bees pollinating

Pollinators such as insects, birds, and bees are selective about the plants they will visit. Therefore, great attention is given to using plants that local pollinators will visit and in minimizing any harm inflicted on them.

POLY HOUSE

(See: Greenhouse)

POME

A fleshy fruit (as an apple or pear) consisting of an outer thickened fleshy layer and a central core with usually five seeds enclosed in a capsule.

POROSITY

The measurement of a material's void or open spaces in relation to its overall mass.

In terms of gardening, porosity usually has to do with soil. Water, air, roots and other substances can easily pass through porous material. As such, you want your soil to be somewhat porous.

You can think of it like a kitchen sponge: it has a size or mass, let's say 4" x 3" x 1", but within that measured space is a lot of void, open area.

POST-EMERGENT HERBICIDE

Herbicide used to control already existing weeds in the garden and lawn.

A gardener must follow all label instructions in order for the product to work, as well as to prevent damage to desirable plants. A *non-selective* herbicide kills herbaceous tissue or damages woody tissue plants that it comes in contact with. A *selective* herbicide kills targeted types of plants without damaging desirable plants. *(See: Pre-Emergent Herbicide)*

POTASSIUM

A macronutrient needed by plants for fruit formation and photosynthesis. (See: Nutrients)

Potassium helps with fruit quality and the reduction of diseases. On the analysis of a fertilizer bag, the third number is K, or percent potassium. If the label indicates that the fertilizer has an analysis of 5-10-10, it means that 10 percent of the total bag weight is potassium.

POTTING MIX

A specially formulated man-made medium for growing plants in containers.

Potting mix is far lighter than topsoil or garden soil. Potting mix often contains ingredients to hold moisture, time-released fertilizers, and  space-and-weight-saving materials such as perlite or vermiculite to keep the soil loose and light. A mix can contain peat, compost and sand. A variety of potting mix formulas are available as well as special blends to meet the nutritional and soil requirements of specific plants, such as violets and cacti.

PREDATOR

Something that exists by preying on other organisms. In the garden: a biological control agent that feeds on the "bad bugs."

Spined soldier bug feasting on ladybeetle larva

In gardening terms, predators are usually a good thing to have around, because they hunt, attack, and kill their prey: those "bad bugs" that are harming your plants One way to reduce the use of pesticides in the garden is to increase your knowledge of biological controls, including predators. If you find a pest on your plant – for instance, an aphid – look around for predators that feed on aphids, such as ladybeetles, syrphid flies, and lacewing larvae. Then you can monitor their progress in cleaning up the aphids. If you do determine that pesticides are necessary, select one that targets the pest rather than a broad-spectrum pesticide that kills everything. You can also add plants that provide shelter, pollen and nectar to your garden that attract and encourage the development of predators.

PRE-EMERGENT HERBICIDE

A weed control product that is put on the soil surface to prevent weeds from growing.

The chemical barrier controls weeds at the germination stage; it won't control existing weeds, so flowerbeds must be weed-free and the product must be applied prior to weed germination. Pre-emergent products control mostly annual weeds. *(See: Post-Emergent Herbicide.)*

PROPAGATE/ PROPAGATION

The reproduction of more plants via seeds, cuttings, bulblets, stolons or runners (to name a few types of propagation).

PROSTRATE

A growth habit, usually of woody plants, where stems arch out and away from the center of the plant but remain closer to the ground.

Unlike groundcovers that always hug the soil closely, prostrate plants have branches that may hover just above ground level. Prostrate plants may have a subtle weeping appearance. *Cotoneaster apiculata* is an example of a prostrate shrub.

PRUNING

The selective removal of plant parts – part of a regular maintenance program on many plants that can reduce growth problems.

Proper pruning will enhance a plant's appearance and health. Improper pruning leads to potential problems as well as aesthetic issues. Reasons for pruning include plant health and pest control, training young plants for future growth, controlling growth, rejuvenating overgrown plants, improving appearance, preventing injury (removing low hanging branches over sidewalks), controlling flowering and fruiting. It is also done to create an unusual or unnatural form of a plant (see Pollarding, Bonsai, Topiary).

PUBESCENT

Having short hairs or downy covering – found on some plants and plant parts.

All plants have tiny pores or openings on their surface called "stomata." The plant breathes or transpires through these tiny holes and may also lose valuable moisture during dry periods and in dry, hot winds. To help plants in more arid areas conserve moisture, plants evolved to have pubescence, which minimizes moisture loss via stomata. The hairs slow down the

Magnolia tree after pruning

Some plants have such an abundance of pubescence that you can easily see the hairs. The soft, down-like surface of some plants is soft to the touch and adds visual interest to the garden; it's a new texture! An example would be *Stachys*, commonly called lamb's ear.

Polystichum acrostichoides (Christmas fern)

dry winds as they pass over the plants' leaves just enough to reduce moisture loss. The tiny hairs also act is teeny, tiny umbrellas, shading the plant from the hot, drying sun. In addition, on some plants, the pubescence keeps insects from feeding on the leaves.

Stachys byzantina (lamb's ear)

QUERCUS to QUICK RELEASE

QUERCUS

The genus for oak, a traditional landscape shade tree.

The genus *Quercus* is native to the Northern Hemisphere with many species, both evergreen and deciduous. The fruit of an oak is an acorn. While most oaks are full-size trees, scrub oaks are smaller, with a shrub-like habit.

QUICK RELEASE

(See: Slow Release Fertilizer)

RAIN BARREL
to RUNOFF

RAIN BARREL

A container that allows a gardener to collect and recycle rainwater.

Rain barrels are used to collect rainwater from the roofs of homes and businesses. This water can then be used to water garden plants.

Harvesting rainwater helps gardeners save water and save money on the water bill, as well as helps to prevent water from moving off of a property, possibly causing pollution of streams and lakes. Be sure to have a cover over the rain barrel to prevent mosquitoes from laying eggs in the standing water.

RAIN GARDEN

A type of garden that is designed to be functional (collecting water runoff) as well as aesthetic.

A rain garden is a small area in a residential landscape that collects the runoff from a rain event and temporarily holds the water, allowing it to soak into the ground slowly as opposed to running down the driveway into the gutter and then the sewer. Rain gardens are located in the landscape so that water is directed

into the garden. Rain gardens should also have an aesthetic component and look good in the landscape. Plants in a rain garden should be able to withstand water for a longer period of time than normal landscape plants; they should be able to tolerate dry summer months as well.

REJUVENATION

The act of pruning or cutting a plant back to the ground or near the ground in order to make it look a little better.

Plants sometimes get a little leggy, lanky, or overgrown and can be rejuvenated. When rejuvenating a plant, make sure you

first find out if the plant can handle severe pruning or cutting back to the ground. For some plants, it might take a 2-3 year process to rejuvenate, while others that grow

Rejuvenate shrubs in the early spring, before new growth begins

quickly can rejuvenate in one season. When rejuvenating shrubs, do this in the early spring prior to the new growth leafing out.

RESISTANT/TOLERANT

Referring to how well a plant either resists or tolerates pests.

A plant that is resistant won't be affected by a specific insect or disease. The resistance can be physical (fuzzy or waxy leaf surfaces) or chemical (enzymes that kill pathogens) characteristics or growth patterns (able to block off disease tissue).

A plant that is tolerant may be affected by the specific insect or disease but won't be impacted to the point of plant decline or eventually death. A tolerant plant can still grow and maintain an acceptable appearance or produce a good crop.

RHIZOMES

Thick, swollen underground stems that usually grow horizontally, just at or below the soil surface.

Plants with rhizomes include *Iris*, lily of the valley (*Convallaria*), ginger, bamboo and *Canna*.

RICH

(See: Soil).

ROOT

(See: Plant: Parts of the Plant).

ROOT FLARE

The part of the trunk at the base where it thickens and roots emerge, or where the roots begin to flare out from the trunk.

When the tree is planted, the root flare should be just at or slightly above the soil line. If the root flare is buried, tissue below ground suffers from a lack of carbon dioxide and oxygen exchange and bark tissue is exposed to constant moisture, which can lead to insect and disease problems.

ROOT ROT

When roots die due to disease or over-watered or waterlogged soils.

Root rot (left), healthy roots (right)

Good air circulation in the area of a plant's root system is critical to its health. Constantly wet roots lack oxygen and are suffocated and begin to decay and die. This problem is very common in house plants, especially those in pots that don't have drainage holes. It occurs in the garden as well. Low areas in the garden, where water naturally funnels and collects, is ideal for water loving plants, rain gardens or even bogs, but not plants that require drier soil.

Special note! In areas with heavy clay soil composition, it is important to prepare planting sites that allow for adequate drainage. Digging a small planting hole in tight, compacted clay soil creates a bathtub effect in which water fills the hole and is held in place by the compacted clay. The remedy is to first test the drainage in the planting area. If the drainage isn't good, consider building your garden beds a bit above grade, fixing the drainage problem, or moving the garden bed completely.

ROOTSTOCK

The lower part of a grafted union
used to create a new plant.
(See: Grafting)

In essence, the root-stock is the roots of the new plant and you graft onto it the "top" (or plant) that will grow to have the ornamental or other desired characteristics. For instance, many crabapples do not perform well if grown with their own roots. So instead, many are grafted onto a rootstock, most typically one that the wholesale trade uses, called the MM111, which is a semi-dwarf rootstock.

ROW COVER

A type of material that is used to cover
plants in the garden.

The material used for row covers can be made of plastics as well as fabric. They can be used in the early spring to cover a vegetable crop to protect it from frost damage. In the summer months, row covers can be used to shade plants from extreme heat. Row covers can also be used to prevent certain insects from either laying eggs or feeding on plants. At the end of the season, they can be used to extend the harvest by protecting the crop from cooler temperatures, sort of like a mini-greenhouse.

Gardeners might also see the term *floating row cover*, which is a type of cover that lies directly on top of the crop. This is usually a lightweight fabric that won't crush plants.

RUNNER

A shoot that grows away from the parent plant, touches the ground, sets roots, and sends out another branch that moves away from the plant to set roots…and so on.

A good example of a plant with runners is strawberries. Runners (also called stolons) form new plants identical to the parent plant. Oftentimes, the established runner can be separated from the parent plant and installed in a new location. This is a natural way in which new plants are created without the need of gardener intervention.

RUNOFF

When water and/or applied materials in water (such as fertilizers) are washed away from the application site and into the surrounding water source.

Depending on how much and where it ends up, runoff ranges from the norm, to inconvenient, to damaging the environment. In commercial production of plants with overhead irrigation, you naturally have excess water, which becomes runoff. Efficient growers have laid out their production areas so runoff is directed to ditches or collection sites, to be cleansed and reused for watering plants. Runoff can also take place on homes sites. Fertilizers (organic and inorganic), road salt, leaves and debris can be included in the runoff water. Runoff is carried by streams, creeks and rivers and deposited into lakes and oceans.

SAND to
SYNTHETIC FERTILIZER

SAND

(See: Soil)

SCREEN/SCREENING

An intentional barrier in the garden, either to block a view or to discourage pests from your plants.

In gardening, the term screen has a couple of meanings. Sometimes, a screen is a landscape plant that can be used to hide an undesirable view. Plants for screens are usually evergreens and are a little taller.

Screening material can be used to prevent pests from damaging plants. For instance, netting is used as a screen to prevent birds from getting into blueberry crops, and row covers are used to prevent cabbage moths from laying their eggs on cabbage and other plants in the family.

SEED/SEEDLING

What gives a flowering plant the ability to reproduce. A seed is the end result of pollination. When life emerges from the seed, the young plant is called a seedling.

Some seeds are as tiny as a pinhead while others are large and tough as nails. Many gardeners enjoy the process and cost savings of starting plants from seeds. An entire garden industry revolves around seeds – from an immense selection

Beet seedlings

of seeds for the home gardener to books, magazines, seed starting kits, grow lamps, and much more. And of course, Mother Nature takes care of her own through various methods of seed dispersal.

SELF-POLLINATING

A plant whose flowers have both male and female parts and do not need pollen from another plant in order to develop fruit.

In self-pollinating plants, the pollen from the stamen (male part) can be transferred to the stigma (female part) of the same flower. In some plants such as soybeans and peanuts, this can occur without outside assistance from, for instance, an insect, bee or bird. Insects can still pollinate these types of plants but if they don't happen upon the flower, there will still be fruit.

SEPALS

(See: Flower)

SHADE

Referring to the amount of sunlight that is blocked from reaching an area or plant.

SHADE IN THE GARDEN

Shade is an interesting component of gardening because of its many levels and intensities. Terms relating to shade can be confusing. Here are a few:

Light shade – an area of the garden that is shaded but still has bright light.

Dappled or filtered shade – when the sunlight filters through a canopy and shifts during the day as the sun moves.

Deep or heavy shade – when no sunlight filters through the canopy of a densely-leaved tree. Grass seed will struggle to grow, but many shade-loving plants can. Thin or prune the tree canopy to allow some sunlight to filter down.

Full shade – where no sunlight reaches the site at all. Full shade can be heavy or light.

Partial or medium shade – having sun just part of the day. As the sun moves through the day, shade may be cast in a certain area of the garden. The location doesn't have sun all day and can be shaded by plants or buildings and structures. Some plants thrive in this location, such as those that prefer early morning sun and afternoon shade to protect them from the heat.

SHADE CLOTH

A lightweight material, usually nylon, that can be placed over a structure to provide shade.

Shade cloths are used in nursery production to cover newly-dug plants to protect them from the heat of the sun as well as over greenhouses to provide cooling. Shade cloths can be purchased to provide varying degrees of shade (i.e., 30 percent shade to 90 percent shade).

SHEARING

Cutting back existing plants with a pair of scissors or hedge trimmers.
(See: Pruning)

Shearing plants is when you take a pair of scissors or hedge trimmers and cut them back. Shearing is sometimes known as "cutting back." The purpose is to rejuvenate plants that have become overgrown, leggy or straggly. Hold the stems and branches in your hand and simply cut about 1/3 to 1/2 of the plant off. Some perennials can be sheared or cut clear back to the ground in order to rejuvenate them after they finish blooming, especially if they have a floppy habit. In a week or more, depending on the plant, new growth will come out and the plant will look much nicer.

SHRUB

A woody plant, smaller than a tree, with several stems or branches arising near the base or at ground level – also sometimes called a bush.

SIDEDRESS

A fertilizing method in which the fertilizer is applied to the sides of the plants.

Sidedressing is done after the plants have germinated and are growing. Dry fertilizer is scattered on both sides of the row approximately six to eight inches from the plant, raked into the soil and watered in after application. The best time to do this is right before a rainfall.

SILT

(See: Soil)

SLOW RELEASE FERTILIZER

A type of fertilizer developed to deliver the nutrients to the plant over a period of time.

Slow release fertilizer is available to a plant in three ways: 1) by slowly dissolving in the soil; 2) by microorganisms releasing nutrients from materials; and 3) through granular materials that have a coating of resin or sulfur that controls the rate of release. The directions on the fertilizer will tell you if the product is slow release and if so, how many days it will last. Always follow label instructions when applying fertilizer.

SOAKER HOSE

A specialized watering hose that allows water to drip or weep out from the hose wall.

Soaker hoses are placed on the ground or slightly below grade. The benefit of using a soaker hose is in its water conservation properties. The water is not projected into the air where much of it is lost to evaporation and wind distribution. Also, the hose can be placed near the plants that need the water, not in empty areas of the garden, thus conserving water while efficiently distributing water to the plants' roots where it is needed most. Because the water escapes from the hose slowly, it is able to soak into the garden, not run off or pool in low spots.

SOD

A piece or section of grass that has the foliage, crowns, roots and soil held together as a unit.

A sod grower raises turfgrass and cuts small squares or rolls of sod to sell to a customer who wants an instant lawn, as opposed to waiting for grass seed to mature. Sod can also be used to fill in bare areas of lawn.

SOFTWOOD

(See: Hardwood)

SOIL

The upper layer of earth in which plants grow.

Let's start with the comment that every agronomist (one who studies soil and production of field crops) tells gardeners: "Soil is not dirt; dirt is what is under your fingernails. Soils provide life for plants!"

Soil has many components and consists of not only solid minerals but also of decaying organisms, living organisms, air, and water. These components include mineral matter in the form of sand, silt and clay, microbes (bacteria, fungi, algae), animals (mammals), insects, organic matter and pore space that is either occupied by water or air. The ideal garden soil contains 45 percent minerals, 30 percent water, 20 percent air and 5 percent organic matter.

Your soil is a natural product of the environment and has taken many years to form. Native soils form from the parent material by action of climate (temperature, wind, and water), native vegetation and microbes. It's important to protect your soils by preventing runoff and erosion.

Many gardeners are not fortunate enough to have the perfect soil and therefore, usually have to add amendments to the soil to improve plant growth.

SOME TERMS RELATING TO SOIL

Clay – The smallest mineral particle in soil, microscopic in size.

Lean – Generally referring to a soil that is low in nutrients.

Loam – Soil that has roughly equal proportions of sand, silt, and clay (but not exactly equal) and is considered ideal garden soil.

Rich – Generally referring to soil that has a lot of nutrients.

Sand – The largest mineral particle in soil; it is visible to the naked eye.

Silt – Mineral particles that are smaller than sand but larger than clay, and are about the size of talc.

Structure – The binding together of soil particles into aggregates or clumps of varying sizes and shapes. Soil structure can be improved by adding organic matter and avoiding unnecessary tilling.

Texture – The relative volume of sand, silt and clay particles in the soil.

Coarse-textured soils have more sand and finely textured soils are mostly clay, or clay and silt mixed. Soil texture affects the water-holding capacity of soil, movement of water through the soil, and ease of cultivation. For instance, a heavy clay soil holds moisture for a longer period of time than a sandy soil.

Tilth – The physical condition of soil in relation to plant growth.

It is the physical condition of the soil as related to the ease of tillage, how easily seedlings germinate, and how easily roots can penetrate the soil.

SOIL HORIZONS

Individual horizontal layers seen by exposing a vertical cross section of soil.

The topmost layer is called the horizon and is referred to as topsoil. If there is a layer of leaf litter and other organic matter, it's called the O horizon. A forest, for instance, would have an O horizon from all of the naturally decaying leaves.

Other horizons include:

B horizon – Subsoil made of more compacted material, often nutrient-rich but lower in organic matter

C horizon – Indicating that the parent material, such as glacial till or lake sediments, has not been altered or is slightly altered – and consists of loosened or unconsolidated material native to the locale

R horizon – Bedrock

These horizons are not always in a set order because of natural processes over a period of time.

SOIL STERILIZATION

The process by which harmful pests (insects, pathogens, weeds) are killed in the soil.

Sterilized soil is used in seed starting where healthy soil medium is desired, as well as in new garden beds or nursery production areas to minimize the growth of weeds.

SOIL TEST

An analysis of a soil sample to determine nutrients, pH and any additional material that might be tested for, like lead.

All gardeners should do a soil test when starting a garden. This is the only way you will know exactly what nutrients are needed in order to have the best crop, flowerbed, lawn, or planting possible. Check with your local county Cooperative Extension office to find out about soil testing in your area.

When taking a soil test of your garden, be sure to take small samples of soil from about 10 to 15 different spots in the garden in order to get a good random sample – about a cup's worth in all. If you just take soil from one location, you won't get a good evaluation of the entire garden or location. Be sure to take the soil sample from the same depth as the roots in the crop that you are growing. For instance, if planting a vegetable garden, take soil from 6 - 8 inches in depth. Let the cup of soil dry out for a day or two before sending it to your lab. They will send results and recommendations on the amendments that might be added for the crop that you are growing.

SOLUBLE SALTS

Minerals dissolved in water.

Excess soluble salts in the soil show up as a crust on the surface of the soil or around drainage holes in a pot. A more common problem with houseplants, soluble salts build up in the soil when plants are watered with tap water that might be high in mineral content. Soluble salts may also accumulate when water is allowed to sit in the saucer. To minimize soluble salt buildup in houseplants, use distilled or rain water. In addition, if salts build up, leach soil by pouring lots of water through the soil and allowing it to drain completely through the pot.

SPECIES

A hierarchical level in plant naming, which describes the genus.

When referring to the Latin names of plants, the species is made up of the genus and specific epithet together. The specific epithet is always used with the genus and helps to further identify plants within the genus. For instance, *Homo* is the genus of humans and *Homo sapiens* is the species.

SPECIMEN PLANT

A plant that is so unique it can stand alone in the landscape as a focal point of interest.

There are some garden plants that work best planted in large numbers within a garden bed or as border plants. Then there are those that are superstars and are meant to stand in the spotlight; these are called specimen plants. Specimen plants often have unique features, such as peeling multi-colored bark, interesting architecture, and beautiful flowers or fine foliage. Some specimen plants are those plants that are difficult to acquire, so having one in the garden deserves noting and singling out to the garden observer.

SPREADER

A tool used to distribute fertilizer.

Spreaders are available in one of two styles: drop or broadcast. Drop spreaders release the smaller-sized fertilizer product through small holes in the reservoir bucket. Drop spreaders are ideal for smaller spaces and where you have to do a lot of maneuvering, such as along walks and gardens beds. Rule of thumb, if your lawn is less than 5,000 square feet, a drop spreader is the best fit.

Broadcast spreaders project or "throw" the fertilizer out and away from the spreader. This is ideal when covering larger areas with few obstacles. It may take a bit of practice to get the  hang of using a broadcast spreader, since maintaining a constant walking pace when pushing the spreader is key to equal coverage. Broadcast spreaders project more fertilizer closer to the spreader, with the amount of material distributed becoming less the farther it is projected. Consult the spreader's operating manual for best practices, such as how much to overlap the broadcast rows to ensure a uniform layer of fertilizer. In addition, if you get a little fertilizer on sidewalks and driveways, be sure to sweep this back into the lawn so that it's not washed into the sewer or tracked into the house.

SPREADING

The growth pattern of a plant that grows out and away from its center and low to the ground – having a "spreading habit" – or a term to describe the growth of a plant based on how wide it might become. Can also refer to a plant that spreads through rhizomes or stolons such as a groundcover or vine. (See: Habit)

SPUR

In trees: a short, stunted branch of a tree that can be almost thorn-like in nature. In flowers: an elongated tube or spike extending from the flower and containing nectar. The spur can be straight or curved, long or short.

If you are working with fruiting trees (ornamental or edible) you are bound to come across this word. Some trees produce flowers and fruits at the tip of

their branches, others on small offshoots or spurs along the length of a branch. Knowing if a tree produces fruit at the branch tip or on spurs is critical to understanding best pruning practices.

Spur-bearing fruit trees (many apples, crabapples and pears) produce far more fruit than their tip-bearing counterparts. Examples of plants with flowers containing spurs: *Aquilegia* (columbine) and *Delphinium* (larkspur).

STAKING

Using external supports to keep plants upright.

Staking is sometimes necessary for plants with floppy habits or in the vegetable garden for tomatoes and climbing plants such as peas. The key to staking is to do it early! Stake plants before they get too tall and flop over, and for maximum production in vegetables. If you put your staking material in the flowerbed early in the season, the plant foliage grows up and around the material, hiding it. If you wait until they plants flop over, you end up using the "choking" method: you gather up the stems, put a rope around them and tie them chokingly to a stake. This is not a pretty picture!

STAMEN

(See: Flower)

STANDARD

Referring to the size of a tree, most often fruiting trees. Other terms for size are semi-dwarf and dwarf. Standard also refers to a specimen plant that has a "feature" plant on top of a trunk or main stem.

Standard is the reference term that we use to refer to the mature natural size of a tree, specifically a fruit tree. Other terms include semi-dwarf and dwarf trees; these are grown on rootstock that reduces the tree's mature size. Trees grafted to semi-dwarf rootstock typically reach 60-90 percent of the standard plant size. Those trees growing on dwarf rootstock only reach 30-60 percent standard size. *(See: Grafting)*

Why is this a good thing? Dwarf and semi-dwarf fruiting trees come to maturity more quickly, producing fruit earlier. Since they are smaller in size, they are easier to harvest, require less pruning and can be used in smaller spaces, such as smaller farms, backyards and even grown in large containers.

Perhaps you have seen some of the fun, different types of specimen plants such as a lilac, cotoneaster or other shrub growing on top of a tree trunk. In this case, standard can also refer to the trunk or "middle portion" of a top-grafted plant. To produce a top-grafted plant you quite often (beginning from bottom to top) have one plant that serves as the rootstock, onto which you've grafted a "standard" or middle stem, and then on top of the standard you've grafted the plant whose ornamental characteristics you want to feature.

STIGMA

The sticky surface at the tip of the female part of the flower (the pistil). The stigma traps and holds the pollen grains.

STOLON/STOLONIFEROUS

A specialized type of horizontal above-ground stem that typically has thinner internodes. Plants that produce stolons are called stoloniferous.

The main plant produces stolons that grow out in several directions. These stolens can eventually root and become new plants. Strawberry plants, for example, send out stolons, often called runners, as they spread across the garden surface.

 These stolons or runners can set roots and form new plants that are identical to the parent plant. They can then be cut and separated from the parent plant. As a result, spreading plants are great for covering larger areas of the garden. One thing to consider: Stoloniferous plants do not necessarily create a dense covering like groundcovers.

STRUCTURE

(See: Soil)

SUBOPPOSITE

(See: Leaf Pattern)

SUCCULENT

A type of plant that has thick, fleshy leaves, stems or tubers.

SUCKERS

Growths that occur on a tree, emerging from its base.

Suckers are vigorous growth that occurs on a tree and come from the base of the tree. These are usually unsightly and should be removed. Do not use chemicals to control suckers, as this can lead to injury  to the tree. Prune them at the base of the tree. Suckers sometimes indicate that a tree is in stress; in other cases, certain species are prone to suckering.

Suckers are also the sprouts that come back after a tree or shrub has been cut at ground level. The tree or shrub is trying to re-grow in order to survive. The only surefire way to get rid of these is to grind out the stump of the plant.

Additionally, suckers are also shoots that emerge a distance from the main trunk. Some species of trees spread by sending up suckers from underground roots that come from the mother plant. There are species of plants that can be propagated by digging up the suckers (separating it from the mother plant) and replanting in a new location.

And finally, you'll hear the term suckers used in reference to tomatoes. Side shoots or suckers form in the axils between the leaf and the stem. Some of these suckers are pruned in order to have better fruit.

SUNSCALD

A type of plant injury caused by exposure to bright sunlight, excessive heat and/or wind.

Sunscald occurs, for instance, on plants that come directly from the greenhouse and are placed outside in the sun without being hardened off first. *(See: Hardening Off)*

SUSCEPTIBLE HOST

A plant that is susceptible to a specific disease or insect. (See: Disease Triangle)

Plant pathogens and insects are host specific and prefer certain plants. A susceptible host is one that has the genetic makeup that permits the development of a particular disease or the attack from a specific insect.

SUSTAINABILITY/ SUSTAINABLE LANDSCAPING

Gardening and landscaping practices adopted by gardeners in response to environmental concerns.

Style, design, function and beauty do not have to be sacrificed when creating a landscape that is in harmony with nature or sustainable. Creating sustainable gardens starts with the design and carries through with material selection, plant placement and maintenance. Sustainable gardens have a positive impact on the environment in that they may reduce water needs by harvesting rain water runoff for future use or using water runoff to maintain a water/rain garden.

Sustainable gardens use integrated pest management, bringing in and creating environments suitable for beneficial insects to combat destructive insects. And, of course, the practice of composting garden waste and kitchen waste is a part of sustainable gardening. This is, by all means, a very limited look at ways in which a garden can be sustainable.

SYMPTOMS

The signs on a plant that there is disease, insect or environmental damage.

Symptoms are results of a disease-causing organism or an insect feeding on a plant.

Hail damage on Hosta

Disease-causing organisms can produce symptoms such as leaf spots, leaf scorch and wilting, distortion, and more. Abiotic or non-living disease symptoms can be a result of poor soil fertility, temperature extremes, and physical damage, among others. Insects lead to symptoms such as holes in leaves, wilting stems (from something boring into the stems), missing plant parts and more.

SYNTHETIC FERTILIZER

Man-made material used to provide additional nutrients to the soil, thus increasing the growth and vigor of plants.

Unlike organic fertilizers, synthetic fertilizers do not contain natural or organic matter. They are generally formulated for specific types of plants, unless they are labeled a general purpose fertilizer. *(See: Fertilizer)*

TAPROOT
to TURF

TAPROOT

The main downward-growing root, with limited branching.

Plants usually have one of two types of root systems - taproot or fibrous. The root is considered the food storage organ for the plant. Plants with taproots include carrots, beets, radishes, parsnips, and dandelions.

TAXONOMY

A classification system.

Taxonomy is one of the most useful classification systems. It's the science of systematically naming and organizing organisms into similar groups with similar characteristics. The characteristics are based on gross morphology or physical characteristics including flower form, leaf shape, buds, fruit form, bark, etc. This system of classification starts at the highest level (kingdom) and divides organisms into groups, all the way down to the species.

TEMPERATE

A geographic area where the climate is not too hot, like the tropics, or not too cold, like the Arctic, but it still experiences four seasons.

Temperate areas have enough variance in temperature to experience four seasons – spring, summer, fall and winter. It's not all a bed of roses though (we had to have at least one garden pun!). Gardeners in temperate areas have to be on their toes! Many temperate-area gardens experience drastic weather conditions such as cold winters and hot summers – think the windy city of Chicago. Also, the weather can change wildly in a week, or even a day. The running joke in Cincinnati, Ohio, is if you don't like today's weather, just wait a day and it will be quite different. If you live in Cleveland, Ohio, wait an hour!

TENDRIL

Modified leaves or branches that can wrap around a fixed object, allowing a plant to grow or climb up the object.

How does the *Wisteria* and sweet pea climb the trellis? Seriously, this is not a chicken crossing the road joke! It climbs with tendrils! These plants will grow up a tree, arbor, shrub or anything else they can wrap their little fingers – we mean tendrils – around.

TERMINAL BUD

A bud that is located at the tip of the stem.

TEXTURE

The visual characteristics of a plant's surface or its structure within the landscape.

Rodgersia

The best way to understand texture is to go outside (with this book in hand) and touch the plants in your garden. What you are feeling as you touch the surface of the plants, the glossy sheen of a southern magnolia, the velvety feel of lamb's ear and the soft, wispy light as air feel of a fine grass is the texture. The texture of a plant also becomes the texture of a garden. A hard, coarse mugo pine is balanced by the softer texture of a tall *Calamagrostis* 'Karl Foerster' ornamental grass. The mood you create in your garden is achieved by selecting plants with textures that emulate that emotion.

THATCH

A tightly interwoven layer of living and dead tissue found between the green grass and the soil surface.

Thatch is made up of old stems, leaf sheaths, and roots that take longer to decay than the grass tissue. A thatch depth greater than ½ inch can lead to problems in the lawn, including disease and insects. It also makes the lawn more susceptible to drought damage. Proper mowing habits that include leaving the grass clippings on the lawn do not contribute to thatch buildup. Potential causes of thatch buildup include: excessive amount of nitrogen fertilizer in the spring, mowing infrequently or allowing the grass to get too tall between mowings, and compacted soil conditions.

THIN/THINNING

Selectively removing some of the newly emerged seedlings to ensure that the remaining plants are able to grow without competition.

It is not always easy to drop seeds in starting mix or garden bed and have them perfectly spaced between each plant, especially when the seed is small. Quite often, the new seedlings will come in as thick as grass, which is not a good thing because they won't have enough room to grow! If you have plants that re-seed freely in the garden, like Brazilian verbena or johnny-jump-ups, you will want to remove a few of the new season's seedlings to make certain you have a stand of healthy, strong, new plants that won't fight each other for space.

From a vegetable garden perspective, if you're direct sowing seeds like carrots, beets or radishes, once they emerge you'll want to go in and remove seedlings in order to provide adequate room for the underground portion of the plants to properly develop. Same goes for larger plants such as green beans. Thin out seedlings to allow for good spacing between plants.

This is always a painful process for gardeners, as we don't want to lose any plants that have germinated. Therefore, make use of those that you pull. For instance, as onions grow, pull every other green onion (and eat!), to give those still in the ground room to grow to a larger, fuller size. That way you have bigger onions you can harvest and store in a cool, dark area and use for cooking during the fall and winter. With lettuce, we like to thin when the plants are very young and use the tiny lettuce plants in a microgreen salad. Nothing goes to waste!

THORN

A stiff, pointed projection from a branch, stem or trunk of a plant.

Thorns can range from quite small to very large. In desert plants, thorns help to conserve water. In other plants, thorns are defense mechanism, protecting the plants from foraging animals.

THRESHOLD

The magnitude of intensity that must be exceeded for a certain reaction or result to occur.

In gardening, the term threshold refers to the amount of damage a plant can handle from a pest. There are several types of thresholds that can be established. For instance, in crop production, an economic threshold is the point in which the pest population causes economic damage to the crop. This usually refers to the size of the pest population. For a gardener, the threshold is how much damage you can personally tolerate before you decide that you should take pest control actions. For instance, one tomato hornworm on our tomato plants is not usually a big problem as it will not cause extensive damage. However, if there were numerous tomato hornworms on our tomatoes eating a lot of foliage and reducing the amount of tomatoes, we have reached our threshold and may want to take action.

THUG

A plant that has the tendency to take over a garden.

Thugs are usually those plants that spread quickly, either by rhizomes (underground stems) or through re-seeding prolifically. Thugs can quickly get out of hand and enter the "weed" classification.

TILL/TILLING

Turning over the soil in your garden or landscape in preparation for planting.

When it comes to preparing a new garden bed for the first time or preparing the garden for planting in the spring, many people turn to tilling with a machine. In addition, there are times we till to work in soil amendments to the garden bed such as pine fines (finely ground pine bark mulch) or compost. Tilling hard, compact soil breaks up the soil, making it easier for water, air and roots to pass through. However, tilling the soil is not always beneficial or necessary, and can be somewhat controversial. You will find different schools of thought when it comes to tilling your garden. Farmers use the technique called no-till in order to prevent erosion and compaction of the soil.

Gardeners are also using no-till as well. However, if you are going to use no-till, you have to make sure that you don't walk on the areas where you will be planting; when you do this, you compact the soil. To reduce soil compaction, create paths between your planting areas that will allow you to reach at least to the center of the planting bed. If you only have room for a single path, it's preferable to have beds that are no more than four feet across.

Each time you till you break up the aggregates that are formed in the soil; no-till allows the aggregates to continue forming, providing a great environment for root growth. Our recommendation is to avoid tilling unless it's necessary and then if you are going to till, do it as little as possible. You can over-till and break down the aggregates and create a really bad soil situation. Don't beat the soil to death with a tiller. Some possible negative effects of tilling are:

Erosion: Excessive tilling, especially on hillsides can cause erosion.

Weeds: Disturbed soil often finds weeds taking hold. If your soil is nutrient rich and well-draining there is no need to tinker with something that is not broken.

Earthworms: Earthworms and other healthy organisms live in the soil and are disturbed when the soil is tilled.

TILTH

(See: Soil)

TISSUE CULTURE

A propagation method used to produce new plants by taking a small culture, or piece of tissue, from a plant to produce more plants within a sterile, controlled environment, such as a lab.

Stage III

Stage III rooted

Stage II

TOPDRESS

To apply fertilizers to the soil's surface after planting.

Topdressing of plants occurs after planting, when fertilizers are applied over the soil and the plant surface. Be sure to wash the fertilizer off of the plants and into the soil after application; otherwise, fertilizer can burn the foliage.

TOPIARY

The age-old practice of pruning, trimming and training vines, trees and shrubs to take on a pre-determined ornamental form of other plants, animals, people and geometric shapes. A topiary is the resulting finished product or plant of this practice.

Some topiaries are quite simple, such as potted ivy trained to grow around a heart-shaped wire. Others utilize evergreens like arborvitae, which are expertly trimmed into shapes. Many can take on fanciful

shapes through pruning and may even depict an entire scene, such as the topiary garden in Columbus, Ohio, which recreates the famous painting by

Georges Seurat: *Sunday Afternoon on the Island of La Grande Jatte.*

Topiary plants can also be started with a wire-formed foundation, which is filled with planting medium and then planted. When a wire form is used, the shape can be extreme and instantly lush – ideal for displays that are changed regularly, such as at amusements parks or show gardens.

TOPPING

Drastically removing or cutting back large branches of mature trees.

Topping is NOT a good practice and can lead to weakened overall branch structure on trees. This leads to rapid new growth, weak limbs, potential increase in insect and disease problems, and shock to the tree among other problems. Topping is quick, easy, and usually a cheaper alternative than hiring a qualified arborist to prune a tree correctly – but it is the wrong choice if you want a strong tree. A qualified arborist will take time to select the right branches to remove without significant damage to tree health. If pruned properly, a tree won't need pruned as often as one that is topped. *(See: Pruning, Pollarding.)*

TOPSOIL

The original upper two inches or so of soil.

Gardeners would love to have this much rich topsoil!

Here, in the top layer of earth, is where most of the rich, organic matter is found, which is comprised of decomposing plants, leaves, fallen trees and even animal waste. In newer neighborhoods, soil is turned, manipulated and redistributed when building homes, roads and utilities, leaving little if any original topsoil on the surface.

TRAILING

Horizontally-growing plants that remain close to the ground.

Plants with horizontal habits have very little (if any) structure to hold them upright, making them ideal groundcovers.

TRANSPLANT

To move a plant from one growing location to another.

Editing the garden is something all gardeners do, perhaps even every year. Many perennials and small shrubs can be easily moved (i.e., transplanted) to a new location in the garden. Plants are moved for aesthetic reasons, to install them in a more suitable growing habitat, or to create or extend a garden. Before you dig, consult your plant guides for

the best time of year to move your plants. The best way to prevent this problem is to have a great landscape design on paper so that you know what goes where in the landscape. Of course, crazy gardeners are always buying new plants and tweaking the garden, so sometimes it just can't be avoided. And of course, before any major digging project, "Know what's below!" Call 811 to have utility lines marked.

TREATED SEED

Seed that has received an application of pesticide designed to reduce, control or repel seed pests.

In an effort to reduce the amount of treatment needed to preserve the health of plants, treated seeds were developed. Treated seed is more likely to grow and thrive resulting in higher crop yields. Always read the label for proper handling of treated seed.

TROPICAL

Plants that originate in climates where there are year-round warm temperatures.

Some tropical plants live in areas with consistently high rainfall; others may be found in areas with periods of great rain as well as drought. Tropical plants are a wonderful addition to the home where

regulating temperature, humidity and water intake is easy. In some warmer climate areas (such as California or Florida) tropical plants

are right at home in the landscape and can survive year-round without special intervention by the gardener. In areas that experience cold winters, tropical plants are grown as garden annuals (we pull them at the end of the season and compost them) or we bring them inside during winter months.

TURF

Another term for lawn or grass.

UNDERCUT
to UPRIGHT

UNDERCUT

Part of a three-step process for pruning limbs that are over 1.5 inches thick.

When branches are small, under 1.5 inches, one pass of the pruners or loppers makes a clean cut. When branches are larger, and require a saw, there is a risk that the weight of the branch that is being removed can pull and rip bark from the larger branch or trunk as it's being cut. To prevent this from happening and to get as clean a cut as possible, an undercut is made first. Moving at least 3 inches away from the main branch or trunk from which the branch is being removed, take the saw and cut up from the underside of the branch 1/3 of the width of said branch. Then, move out farther from the main branch or trunk, a little past the first cut, and cut down into the branch, passing

all the way through. Should the weight of the falling limb begin to tear the bark, the undercut will stop the falling branch and prevent it from damaging the tree. The final cut is at the branch collar.

Additionally, undercutting is also the process of trimming the roots of trees while they remain in the ground in a production growing field. Undercutting liner (baby) trees, before digging for sale, and while in the field, promotes a bigger fibrous root system. Harvesting of bareroot liner trees can sometimes be referred to as undercutting, as well.

UNDERSTOCK

A plant with roots onto which the new top plant or scion is grafted.

There are various reasons why an understock may need to be utilized in the plant propagation process. For instance, some plants do not propagate well by cuttings or they produce an inferior root stock (like shallow roots which means they can easily blow over during a wind storm). Another example is using certain understock plant species when grafting apple trees. The understock may cause dwarfing of the top part of the plant, resulting in a dwarf apple tree.

Thus, an understock and its root system generally has more desirable characteristics than the top part of the plant (or scion) could produce on its own. *(See: Budding, Grafting)*

UPRIGHT

Referring to plants whose branches grow upward.

Unlike weeping trees with branches that bend and reach towards the ground, upright plants have branches that are outstretched as the plant grows vertically, and may even have branches that reach up towards the sky; an example would be a dawn redwood. You might also see the term upright arching, which means the plant grows upright and the ends of the branches fall off into an arching habit. A *Forsythia* is an example of an upright arching plant. *(See: Habit)*

VARIEGATED
to VOLUME

VARIEGATED

A plant whose foliage is marked with one or more colors.

Variegated leaves can be striped, speckled, blotched, flecked or include a border of one color along the leaf margin, with the inside of the leaf being a different color. Variegated leaves can add visual interest to the garden as well as help brighten dark shade garden areas. Flowers only last so long, but variegated leaves give color throughout the growing season!

VASCULAR SYSTEM

The plant's system of transporting water, nutrients and more throughout the plant.

Higher plants or those with roots (the bottom) and trunks and stems (the top) are considered vascular plants

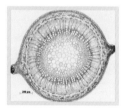

and possess a vascular system that is made up of the xylem and phloem or the conducting elements of these plants. The xylem is responsible for transporting water and nutrients from the roots to the shoots, leaves, and above-ground parts. The phloem is responsible for transporting sugars that are manufactured in the leaves (through the process of photosynthesis) to the roots and other parts of the plant.

VEGETABLE

*A plant grown most often
for food production.*

Vegetable plants, such as carrots, celery, beets and broccoli have edible parts, which, unlike fruits, lack seeds. Vegetables can be eaten cooked and at times, raw.

Celery

VEGETATIVE

The leaf-producing stage of a plant.

The vegetative growth stage of the plant is the period of time when a plant is producing leaves. This occurs after germination and before flowering.

VERMICULITE

*A mineral that expands greatly
when heated and that retains water,
making it quite useful in many
gardening applications.*

When mixed with peat and composted bark, vermiculite creates a growing medium that is ideally suited for seed starting. The soilless mix allows for ample air circulation and the water retention properties of the vermiculite help prevent the seeds from drying out. Bulbs and tubers that are stored over winter are often placed in vermiculite to absorb any excess moisture; thus reduces mold, mildew and bulb rot. When added to heavy clay soils, garden beds and potting soil, vermiculite helps to loosen the soil to allow for more air and water circulation, thus promoting root growth.

VINES

Plants that have little or no support structure, but are able to grow vertically by climbing on other sturdier plants or structures.

By using tendrils (think fingers), or modified branches, vines are able to grasp onto a support structure, hold fast and continue to grow up, out and around.

VITICULTURE

The study of grapes, their growth, cultivation, development and production.

Let's raise a glass to those who study grape production…cheers!

VOLCANO MULCHING

A bad technique for mulching around trees.

For the life of us, we can't figure out where or why this practice started. We wish it would go away, so starting with you, please change this practice! This term was coined to represent the type of mulching that occurs when mulch is piled high up around the trunk of a tree, resembling a volcano, Mulch should never touch the crown or trunk of the plant (unless it's being used for winter protection, then it's removed in the spring before growth resumes). And you only need about two to four inches of mulch around plants.

VOLUME

The amount of soil a container pot holds.

A generic definition of volume is the amount of space within a defined area that can be filled with liquid, gasses, or solids. In regard to plants, volume is the level of soil in a container pot.

WARM SEASON CROPS
to WOUND

WARM SEASON CROPS

Plants that thrive when grown in warm air and soil temperatures.

Some plants, particularly edibles, do best when the air and soil are warm. Melons, tomatoes, beans, corn and cucumbers are warm season plants. The opposite is cool season crops, such as broccoli, cauliflower and cabbage.

WATER IN

To provide water to a newly installed plant.

Watering-in is a term used to describe adding water to a newly installed plant. The water settles the new planting area (removes air pockets and defines any unwanted low spots in the planting area) and ensures the new plant has adequate water to help it transition to its new location.

Keep in mind, these newly established plants are going to require a little more water in the beginning to get them established.

WATER SOLUBLE

Any solid substance that dissolves when in contact with water.

WATERING

Manually adding moisture to the garden, lawn or potted plants to supplement low rainfall.

This garden chore is done with a watering can, garden hose with sprinkler or nozzle, or a soaker hose. It can also refer to providing moisture to indoor plants. *(See: Irrigation)*

WATERSPROUTS

Vigorous shoots of growth on woody trees that usually occur on branches.
(See: Suckers)

Watersprouts have a tendency to grow straight up and become really tall; they are also usually vegetative and won't produce fruit. If watersprouts aren't pruned out *(See: Pruning)*, they eventually get so big that they clog up the center of the tree, preventing light from penetrating. This is especially important in fruit production.

WATER WISE

The conservative, thoughtful use of water in your garden.

THE WATER-WISE GARDEN

There are several measures you can take to incorporate water-wise gardening in your garden. With water-wise gardens we start with planning gardens that are less water dependent, and we look at ways to most efficiently and conservatively water plants.

- Start with good bed preparation so that your plants have the best chance to really get established.

Prepare the garden bed with rich organic soil and finish the planting with a layer of mulch.

Sandy soil dries out more quickly and mulch conserves water usage while reducing weed germination, a nice bonus.

- Select the best plant for the job.

If you plan to work with sandy soil, select plants that thrive in such soil. If you add plants that require steady soil moisture to your sandy soil garden, it will mean a lot of additional watering and fertilizing.

- Use soaker hoses and do spot watering.

Only water those plants that need it and direct all water to the plants and their roots.

- Use rain barrels, and plant rain gardens.

- Utilize good lawn care practices that produce a thick turf that will withstand a few weeks of dry weather.

- Add a deck or patio in areas where you like to gather for conversation and meals.

Why struggle to keep a lawn looking good in a high traffic area? A patio requires no water, leaves more time for fun and is a great place to add container plantings.

WEED

An undesirable plant; or a plant that is out of place – depending on your point of view.

People have a tendency to define weeds in many different ways. No matter the terminology, weeds continue to give gardeners headaches! One of the best ways to control weeds in your garden is to keep them from going to seed. Once they go to seed, you just have that much more work the next year.

WEEPING

A plant whose side branches gently arch away from the center leader and cascade downward.

Sometimes the branches of weeping trees are left undisturbed and reach the ground. Other times the branches are pruned like bangs in a haircut. Neither way is right or wrong, it is simply a matter of personal preference.

WHORLED

(See: Leaf Pattern)

WICK/WICKING

The ability of a liquid to flow in opposition to gravity through narrow spaces.

Wicking, or capillary action, can occur if a plant is grown in a peat pot and then planted in the ground with some of the peat pot above ground, exposed to wind and elements. Water will move up or "wick" through the peat pot and away from the root system, leading to the roots drying out quicker.

WILDLIFE

All non-domesticated and feral animals native to the area, such as songbirds, birds of prey, rodents, mammals and other creatures.

WILT

A condition that occurs when a plant loses rigidity, resulting in herbaceous stems or leaves becoming limp, flaccid or droopy.

At left, wilted leaves... and leaves after watering.

Wilt occurs when the rate of absorption of water by the roots is slower than the rate of loss of water through the leaves. A plant can have damp soil and still be wilted when it is first planted and the roots haven't established. For instance, a young tomato seedling planted on a hot, sunny day and watered in thoroughly might wilt during the heat of the day and perk back up at night when it's cooler. A plant can be in waterlogged soil and wilt, as well. In this case, it's due to the lack of oxygen in the soil that leads to damaged roots that can't absorb moisture. The first rule of thumb with a wilted plant is to check the soil.

WINTER INTEREST

Plants, hardscapes, art and other features that are visually interesting in the winter garden when most plants are dormant or after annuals have been removed.

Along with continuous blooms, winter interest may be one of the more difficult aspects of design for new gardeners to master. Winter interest starts from the ground up: paths, whether curved or formally laid out, when defined by edging, add shape and pattern in the winter garden. Shrubs, grasses, perennials with interesting seed heads and architecturally interesting small trees also are quite beautiful in the winter. The grasses add movement and look stunning with a light frost; and trees, especially those with dramatic branches, are wonderful to look at with or without a blanket of snow. Benches, urns, birdbaths, and garden structures like a gracefully arched arbor,

are focal points in the winter garden. Usually surrounded by plants, in the winter garden structures and art stand out on their own, taking center stage.

Don't panic and think that your entire landscape has to have winter interest. Take a look at those areas that are seen the most during the winter that would be considered priority areas. For instance, where do you spend most of your time in the winter? Look out those windows and try to develop that part of your garden for winter interest.

WOODY

Describing a woody plant or one that has woody tissue structure for the stems, but doesn't die back to the ground.

Some herbaceous plants have stems that are woody but they are not classified as woody plants. This gets a little confusing, but keep in mind that trees and shrubs are considered woody plants and perennials are considered herbaceous plants. It gets a little more confusing when a plant such as lantana is considered an annual in the northern U.S. and a perennial or shrub in the South. How you might classify a plant in terms of woody, herbaceous, annual or perennial sometimes depends on your geographical region.

WOUND

The result of damage to any part of a plant.

Wounding of plants occurs in a variety of ways, one of them being intentional pruning. However, if you make the proper pruning cut, the wound will close properly and the potential for problems decreases. Other causes of wounding to plants include wind damage, hail, lawnmower and other lawn equipment, animals, and more. The sites of the wound can possibly lead to disease and insect issues for

the plant, so try to keep plants as healthy as possible.

XERISCAPING
to XYLEM

XERISCAPING

Designing a landscape and/or garden with the purpose of reducing or eliminating the need for irrigation or additional water to keep plants alive.

Xeriscaping is common in areas of the North America where access to water is limited. The plants used are those that thrive in that type of climate. Other terms that are sometimes used interchangeably for xeriscaping include smart gardening, water-conserving landscaping, drought-tolerant gardening or water-wise gardening.

XYLEM

The part of the vascular system responsible for transporting water and nutrients from the roots throughout the plant to the shoots, leaves, and above-ground parts. (See: Cambium.)

The vascular systems (xylem and phloem) are different in certain groupings of plants. In dicots or plants with two cotyledons (the first leaves that appear when a plant germinates) the xylem and phloem are arranged in a ring, allowing for the stem to grow in girth. In a monocots or plants with one cotyledon, the vascular system has conducting tubes scattered throughout the stem. *Note:* cotyledons are stored food and what the newly germinating seed needs to get growing.

YELLOWING

YELLOWING

When the foliage or leaves of a plant that are normally green begin to turn yellow.

This term is often used when referring to a plant problem. Nutrient deficiencies as well as pest problems such as insect or disease damage can lead to leaves turning yellow. However, as in the case with the photo to the left, this is normal needle yellowing that occurs on evergreens. As mentioned in the broadleaved evergreen definition, these types of plants don't keep their leaves or needles forever. When it comes time to drop their older needles, they tend to turn yellow. If the yellowing occurs on the inner needles or leaves, this is normal. Identify the main cause of the problem before taking action.

Aldo Leopold, author of *A Sand County Almanac*, whose work has had lasting influence on natural resource management and policy, says it best:

"Pines have earned the reputation of being 'evergreen' by the same device that governments use to achieve the appearance of perpetuity: overlapping terms of office. By taking on new needles on the new growth of each year, and discarding old needles at longer intervals, they have led the casual onlooker to believe that needles remain forever green.

"Each species of pine [and spruce, and fir, etc.] has it own constitution, which prescribes a term of office for needles appropriate for its way of life. Thus the white pine retains its needles for a year and a half; the red and the jack pine for two years and a half. Incoming needles take office each June and outgoing needles write their farewell addresses in October. All write the same thing, in the same tawny yellow ink, which by November turn brown. Then the needles fall, and are filed in the duff to enrich the wisdom of the stand. It is this accumulated wisdom that hushes the footsteps of whoever walks under the pines."

ZONE

ZONE

A geographic area defined by average winter (or summer) temperature.

North America is divided into geographic areas defined not by longitude and latitude, but by average annual minimum winter temperature. Each zone is 10 degrees warmer or colder than the neighboring zone. The zones (often broken

into sub zones) are used by gardeners to determine which plants will grow best in their garden. The lower the zone number, the colder the average minimum winter temperature. In the United States, there are 13 zones, with 1 being the coldest and 13 the warmest. In Canada, the zones range from 1 through 9a,

which reflects the lack of the warmest climate areas.

Zones do not have set boundaries. In some areas, consistently warmer weather patterns have warranted updated (and higher) zone numbers.
(See: Hardiness/Hardy)

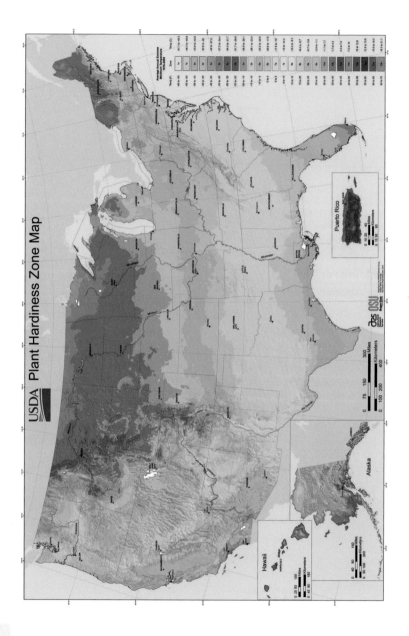

USDA Plant Hardiness Zone Map

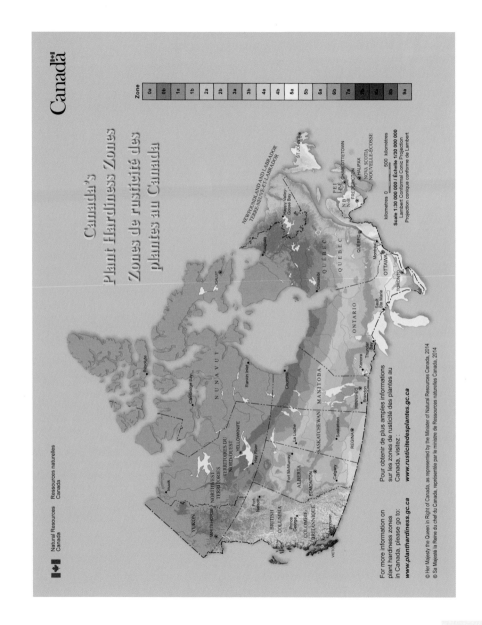

Natural Resources
Canada

Ressources naturelles
Canada

Canada's
Plant Hardiness Zones
Zones de rusticité des
plantes au Canada

Zone
0a
0b
1a
1b
2a
2b
3a
3b
4a
4b
5a
5b
6a
6b
7a
7b
8a
8b
9a

For more information on
plant hardiness zones
in Canada, please go to:
www.planthardiness.gc.ca

Pour obtenir de plus amples informations
sur les zones de rusticité des plantes au
Canada, visitez :
www.rusticitedesplantes.gc.ca

© Her Majesty the Queen in Right of Canada, as represented by the Minister of Natural Resources Canada, 2014
© Sa Majesté la Reine du chef du Canada, représentée par le ministre de Ressources naturelles Canada, 2014

kilometres 0   500 kilomètres
Scale 1:30 000 000 / Échelle 1/30 000 000
Lambert Conformal Conic Projection
Projection conique conforme de Lambert

RESOURCES

To our readers: This resource list is by no means comprehensive! But it does provide you with some of the go-to resources that we use when it comes time to look something up. We have tried to select those that would apply to a wide geographical audience.

There are lots of books that focus on plants that grow best in your region but we couldn't include all of them. We have also listed websites and apps, aware that they may disappear at some point; but the ones shown below have been around awhile. In addition, we did not mean to slight anyone in the gardening world by not listing a resource – and we hope you understand that there just wasn't enough room for all!

BOOKS

The American Horticultural Society A-Z Encyclopedia, Christopher Brickell. DK Adult, 2011

American Horticultural Society Plant Propagation: The Fully Illustrated Plant-by-Plant Manual of Practical Techniques, Alan Toogood. DK Adult, 1999.

American Horticultural Society Pruning and Training, Christopher Brickell, David Joyce. DK Adult, 2011.

Armitage's Garden Perennials, 2nd ed., Allan M. Armitage. Timber Press, 2011.

Armitage's Native Plants for North American Gardens, Allan M. Armitage. Timber Press, 2006.

Armitage's Vines and Climbers: A Gardener's Guide to the Best Vertical Plants, Allan M. Armitage. Timber Press, 2010.

The BackPocket Gardener, The Ohio Nursery & Landscape Association and The Ohio State University Extension. Available through www.onla.org.

Botany for Gardeners: Third Edition, Brian Capon. Timber Press, 2010

Garden Insects of North America (Princeton Field Guides), Whitney Cranshaw. Princeton Univ. Press, 2004.

Gardener's Latin: Discovering the Origins, Lore and Meanings of Botanical Names, Bill Neal. Robert Hale, Ltd., 1993

Herbaceous Perennial Plants: A Treatise on their Identification, Culture and Garden Attributes, 3rd ed., Allan M. Armitage. Stipes, 2008.

Manual of Herbaceous Ornamental Plants, 4th ed., Steven M. Still. Stipes, 1993.

Manual of Woody Landscape Plants: Their Identification, Ornamental Characteristics, Culture, Propagation and Uses, 6th ed., Michael A. Dirr. Stipes, 2009.

National Wildlife Federation Field Guide to Wildflowers of North America, David Brandenburg, Craig Tufts, 2010.

Newcomb's Wildflower Guide, Lawrence Newcomb. Little, Brown and Company, 1989.

The North American Guide to Common Poisonous Plants and Mushrooms of North America, Nancy Turner, Patrick Aderkas. Timber Press, 2009.

Pests and Diseases: The Complete Guide to Preventing, Identifying, and Treating Plant Problems (American Horticultural Society Guide), Pippa Greenwood, Andrew Halstead, A.R. Chase, Daniel Gilrein. DK Adult, 2000.

Practical Botany for Gardeners: Over 3,000 Botanical Terms Explained and Explored, Geoff Hodge. University of Chicago Press, 2013.

Taylor's Encyclopedia of Garden Plants: The Most Authoritative Guide to the Best Flowers, Trees, and Shrubs for North American Gardens, Frances Tenenbaum. Houghton Mifflin Harcourt, 2003.

WEBSITES

General:

eXtension.org (find any land grant university Extension office in your area at this site as well as gardening resources)

American Distance Education Consortium – E-Answers
http://e-answers.adec.edu/

American Horticultural Society
www.ahs.org

American Public Gardens Association
www.publicgardens.org

The Missouri Botanical Garden,
www.missouribotanicalgarden.org

The National Garden Bureau,
www.ngb.org

National Sustainable Agriculture
Information Service
http://attra.ncat.org/

The Royal Horticultural Society
www.rhs.org.uk

Searchedu.com
http://searchedu.com. This is a
comprehensive search engine

Plant Databases:

Plant Places
www.plantplaces.com

PLANTS Database
http://plants.usda.gov

University of Connecticut Plant Database
www.hort.uconn.edu/plants

Insects, Pest & Weed Management, Plant Diseases:

Bug Guide
http://bugguide.net/node.view/15740

Insect ID
www.entomology.wisc.edu/insectid/index.
html

National Pesticide Information Center
Fact Sheets
http://npic.orst.edu/npicfact.htm

North American Insects and Spiders
http://www.cirrusimage.com/

Pesticide Action Network Pesticide Database
http://pesticideinfo.org/Index.html

Vegetable Insects and Their Management
http://extension.entm.purdue.edu/veg

Vegetable MD Online (Cornell University)
http://vegetablemdonline.ppath.cornell.edu/
Home.htm

Weed Identification and Management
www.weedid.wisc.edu/weedid.php

Plant Organizations and Societies:

American Dahlia Society
www.dahlia.org

American Bonsai Association
www.absbonsai.org

American Daffodil Society
www.daffodilusa.org

American Hosta Society
www.americanhostasociety.org

American Hydrangea Society
www.americanhydrangeasociety.org

American Iris Society
www.irises.org

American Orchid Society
www.aos.org

American Rose Society
www.ars.org
www.rose.org

Bulb Society
www.bulbsociety.org

The Garden Club of America
www.gcamerica.org

The Herb Society of America
www.herbsociety.org

National Chrysanthemum Association
www.mums.org

Perennial Plant Association
www.perennialplant.org/

Apps:

Armitage's Greatest Perennials & Annuals, Allan M. Armitage. Sutro Media.

Awesome Insects, Timothy J. Gibb, Phil Abbott. Purdue University.

Dirr's Tree and Shrub Finder, Michael A. Dirr. Timber Press, Inc.

Foolproof Plants for Small Gardens, Susan Morrison. Sutro Media

Leafsnap: An Electronic Field Guide. Created by researchers from Columbia University, University of Maryland, and the Smithsonian Institution.

Purdue Annual Doctor, Cliff Sadof, Janna Beckerman. Purdue University.

Purdue Perennial Doctor, Cliff Sadof, Janna Beckerman. Purdue University.

Purdue Tree Doctor, Cliff Sadof, Janna Beckerman. Purdue University.

Taking Care of Your Yard: The Homeowner's Essential Guide to Lawns, Trees, Shrubs, and Garden Flowers, Mary Welch-Keesey. Purdue University.

Hardiness Zone Maps:

USDA Hardiness Zone Map
http://planthardiness.ars.usda.gov/ PHZMWeb/ <http://planthardiness.ars.usda. gov/PHZMWeb/>

Canadian Hardiness Zone Map
http://www.planthardiness.gc.ca/ <http://www.planthardiness.gc.ca/>

American Horticultural Society
Heat Zone Map
This is an excellent resource for determining the heat tolerance of plants, a companion tool to the hardiness zone maps.
http://www.ahs.org/gardening-resources/ gardening-maps/heat-zone-map

ACKNOWLEDGMENTS

Pam:

To Jim Chatfield, for inspiring me to want to dig deeper and learn more. Jim has always taught my Master Gardener Volunteer incoming first class and likes to tell the new volunteers that you never "master" gardening, but we continue trying by absorbing as much knowledge as possible.

To Denise Johnson, for her always-positive can-do attitude, her never-ending idea-generating mind, and her love of working with Master Gardener Volunteers.

To Linda McCann, for her "what can I do to help" philosophy toward life. Thanks for going through all of the old gardening dictionaries and sorting out the beginning terms for this book.

To my co-workers Carolyn Allen, Jo Brown and Kathy McConkey – you have been supportive of me in every step of my Extension career. I can only hope that I have helped you to grow as much as you have helped. We make a darn good team.

And to the Master Gardeners of Clark County, Ohio – you make my job such a joy. Thanks to all past and current volunteers for your dedication and commitment to Ohio State University Extension and the MGV program.

Maria:

To Dawn Hummel, my BFF and sister in a previous life, for lifting me up in a multitude of ways to reach new professional heights.

To Jenny Koester Smith, without whom I could never have written this book. It was karma that had our career paths reconnect at just the write (another intended bad pun from me) time. Thank you for all your help in providing research and laying a solid foundation for me to build upon.

To my son, Robert Pettorini, for picking up the pieces on other work-related projects and being Grandpa's right hand man, which allowed me to squeeze in this book to my stupidly busy (but rewarding) work load that always seems to overflow. To my Aunt Pat Zampini, for always being there and supporting me in countless ways. You are a rock and one of the strongest women ever!

To Todd Davis, for choosing me as the "Ohio Guest Editor" for *Nursery Management* magazine and giving me the writing bug. To Sally Benson of American Nurseryman and Patty Craft of *Horticulture* magazine, for seeing my potential and providing such wonderful opportunities for me to expand my writing wings and for helping me re-birth my professional career; you helped me get my mojo back!

To Keri Butler, Josh Schneider and Linda Guy, for encouraging me to practice yoga, which helped me learn to "breathe" and maintain my sanity in my wild and crazy world, in particular as book deadlines loomed. And lastly, to the wonderful ladies at Branches of Wellness in Fairport Harbor, Ohio (Erin, Lyndsey, Anna and Michelle), for always providing a positive, healing and nurturing environment that renews me and keeps this "Energizer Bunny" going!

From both of us:

We both thank all of our many horti-culture colleagues who have helped to mold our careers and make us the strong women in horticulture that we are today! Thank you also to Cathy, Holly, Paul and all of the others at St. Lynn's Press who held our hands while we walked through the *Garden-pedia*.

ABOUT the AUTHORS
Pam Bennett

When I graduated from high school I really wasn't sure what I wanted to do for a career. I loved to teach, so I went to Miami University in Ohio to become a physical ed teacher. However, in the summer between my freshman and sophomore year, my mom got me a job. Of course, that's what moms do when their children aren't really motivated to work during the summer, right? It turned out that that summer job in a local garden center in Springfield, Ohio, set me on a new career path.

Since Miami didn't have a horticulture program, I transferred to The Ohio State University and graduated with a Bachelor of Science degree in landscape horticulture. I went back to Springfield and worked in a local garden center and learned so much from my co-workers, especially friend and mentor Marshall Goodfellow. When the position opened in Extension in Clark County for a horticulture program assistant, I jumped at the chance to combine teaching and horticulture. I now have the best job in the entire world! I am currently on track to become an Assistant Professor and have a split position. Half of my Ohio State University Extension job is serving as the horticulture educator in Clark County, Ohio, and the other half is to provide leadership to the state Master Gardener Volunteer program. My volunteer management skills serve me well when I work with MGVs. They are a very special group of people who make my work so enjoyable.

I wear a number of hats, but nothing makes me happier than teaching others about plants – giving presentations about plants and gardening, speaking to audiences eager to learn; I have had the privilege of doing this internationally, nationally and in Ohio. I also write, including for a variety of Extension publications, as well as radio, TV and social media – and I have won a few awards for my creative work along the way.

When I am not on the job, it might seem like I am still on the job. At home, I am always outside in my garden, even sometimes in the rain and cold. I learn so much from my garden at home. I also enjoy baking, hiking, camping, quilting and reading.

Follow me on Facebook at www.facebook.com/osuemgvs; Twitter @osumgv and Instagram at pjbennett14.

ABOUT the AUTHORS
Maria Zampini

I'm a fourth generation nurseryman and proud of it! I grew up on family nursery that was located in Lake County, Ohio, once the Nursery Capital of the World! And while my dad encouraged me to consider other careers, following in the tradition of my forefathers only seemed natural. If I didn't know better, I'd swear my blood runs green!

After graduating with a Bachelor of Science from The Pennsylvania State University, I worked my way up the business and horticultural industry ladders. I am now the president and owner of UpShoot LLC, a boutique horticultural marketing firm specializing in bringing new plant introductions to market, as well as garden-related products.

I'm also the Director of Plant Development for the HGTV HOME Plant Collection. I'm the resident plant geek, sourcing the latest and greatest plant genetics from around the world for the most trusted name in home and gardening: HGTV.

Additionally, this type-A personality writes regularly for many consumer magazines and industry trade journals. I also lecture nationally and internationally on a variety of gardening topics.

When I'm not being a hortaholic, I love my life in Northeast Ohio, living along the shores of Lake Erie. I'm proudly involved in my community and many green industry

associations, but I relish free time when I can, enjoying the beach in Fairport Harbor, practicing yoga and taking long walks with my four-legged friends Belle and Whitey.

To learn more about me, my company UpShoot and how we're "Living,

Supporting & Sharing Horticulture" each and every day, please visit our website at www.Upshoothort.com. You can follow me along the gardening trail on almost all social media platforms under Maria Zampini or UpShoot.

PHOTO CREDITS

A

Accent/Specimen – Pamela Bennett
Acid-loving plants – Holly Rosborough
Aggregate – Joseph Boggs
Agriculture – Holly Rosborough
Alternate – Pamela Bennett
Angiosperm – Jenny Koester Smith
Annuals – Pamela Bennett
Arbor – Holly Rosborough (p.6), Pamela Bennett (p.7)
Aromatic/Fragrant – John Lewis, JLPN, Inc.
Ascending – Pamela Bennett

B

Balled & Burlapped – Jenny Koester Smith
Bare Root – John Lewis, JLPN
Bark – Pamela Bennett
Bedding Plants – Jenny Koester Smith
Beneficials – Danae Wolfe
Biological control – Danae Wolfe
Bloom – Jenny Koester Smith
Bolt/Bolting: Pamela Bennett
Bonsai – Jenny Koester Smith
Border/Border Plant – Holly Rosborough (top), Pamela Bennett (bottom)

Bramble – Ron Wilson
Branch Collar – Pamela Bennett
Broadleaved Evergreens – Jenny Koester Smith (p.14), Botteville [Creative Commons] (p.15)
Bud – Pamela Bennett
Budding – Pamela Bennett (p.16), Holly Rosborough (p.17)
Bulb – Jenny Koester Smith (p.18), Holly Rosborough (p.19)
Bush – Pamela Bennett

C

Cane – Pamela Bennett
Carnivorous Plant – Jenny Koester Smith (p.20-21)
Chipping – Jenny Koester Smith (p.22), Pam Bennett (p.23)
Chlorophyll – Holly Rosborough (p.25)
Chlorosis – Pamela Bennett
Climbing – Jenny Koester Smith
Coir – Pamela Bennett
Cold Frame – Pamela Bennett
Community Garden – Holly Rosborough
Companion Plants – Holly Rosborough

GARDEN TERMS LIST